Cormac McCarthy's
All the Pretty Horses

CONTINUUM CONTEMPORARIES

Also available in this series:

Forthcoming in this series:

· **CORMAC MCCARTHY'S**

All the Pretty Horses

A READER'S GUIDE

STEPHEN TATUM

CONTINUUM | NEW YORK | LONDON

2002

The Continuum International Publishing Group Inc
370 Lexington Avenue, New York, NY 10017

The Continuum International Publishing Group Ltd
The Tower Building, 11 York Road, London SE1 7NX

www.continuumbooks.com

Printed in the United States of America

Library of Congress Cataloging-in-Publication Data

Tatum, Stephen, 1949–
    Cormac McCarthy's All the pretty horses : a reader's guide / Stephen Tatum.
        p. cm. — (Continuum contemporaries)
    Includes bibliographical references.
    ISBN 0-8264-5246-9 (alk. paper)
        1. McCarthy, Cormac, 1933– All the pretty horses. 2. Mexican–American
    Border Region—In literature. 3. Western stories—History and criticism. I. Title.
    II. Series.

PS3563.C337 A79 2002
813'.54—dc21
                                                                2001047751

    ISBN 0–8264–5246–9

Contents

for Kathy

Acknowledgments

In preparing this book I have benefited from the invaluable research assistance of Kelly Jeppson and Kindra Briggs. My thanks to the University Research Committee and the Department of English at the University of Utah for funds to support this research and this project. I also want to extend my gratitude to Dean Rehberger, Andrew Hoffman, Bob Clark, and Susan Kollin for their helpful comments and encouragement along the way. I am grateful to Tom Pilkington and Melody Graulich for accepting for publication some of my earlier thoughts on Cormac McCarthy. Finally, with utmost gratitude and respect, I dedicate this book to the most important person in my life, Kathryn Kingdon Tatum.

The Novelist

I was always attracted to people who enjoyed a perilous life style.

—CORMAC MCCARTHY

Cormac McCarthy does not promote his books the way writers and publishers usually do today. He does not do media appearances or publicity tours. When his books do appear in print—and they have done so at heroically irregular intervals over the past three decades—he neither performs public readings nor signs copies at local bookstores. He does not attend award ceremonies or banquets to receive any honors his writing might receive. He does not write blurbs for or do reviews of other writers' books. Should offers to teach in higher education or writers' workshop settings materialize, he turns them down. Although he finally agreed in the spring of 1992, after some urging by his agent and publisher, to do his first interview to help promote *All the Pretty Horses*, he has vowed never to do another one. As far as McCarthy is concerned, his body of writing—eight novels, a screenplay, and a play—provides all the evidence anyone should need to know about him or his concerns. As novelist Madison Smartt Bell noted in his review of *All the Pretty Horses* for the *New York Times Book Review*, throughout his career McCarthy has "shunned publicity so effectively he wasn't even famous for it."

Given McCarthy's fierce desire for privacy and his corresponding distaste for self-promotion, perhaps it is not too surprising to learn that his five novels published prior to the May 1992 release of *All the Pretty Horses* never sold more than 5,000 hardback copies apiece. Even so, his writing over nearly three decades did usually receive favorable critical notices, did eventually command the respect of his writer peers, and did develop a small, but nevertheless devoted coterie of both academic and general readers. One result: McCarthy became labeled a "writer's writer." His loyal readers and regular reviewers routinely compared his brilliant, yet dark and often disturbing fiction to such major writers as Melville, Faulkner, Joyce, and Hemingway. But given his first five novels' meager sales record, this label was further elaborated to the point that McCarthy was also identified as "the best kept secret in American writing," "the best unknown writer in America," "the best writer you've never read," or "the Invisible Man of American letters." "Unknown" or "invisible" enough to the point that in 1986 — only six years before *All the Pretty Horses* was published — the Ecco Press reprinted McCarthy's first five novels in its "Neglected Books of the 20th Century" paperback series. "Unknown" or "invisible" enough for *Esquire* magazine to preface its pre-publication excerpt from *All the Pretty Horses* with a few of the rumors that swirled around the reclusive McCarthy: that he lived under an abandoned oil derrick in west Texas; that he never talks; that he has worked as a ditch digger and a long-distance trucker; that his fictional characters' nomadic wanderings and loony actions are autobiographical facts.

McCarthy's relative obscurity of course dramatically changed when *All the Pretty Horses* became an immediate bestseller during the late spring and summer of 1992 and also received both the National Book Award and the National Book Critics Circle awards for fiction within its first year of publication. Before the commercial and critical success of *All the Pretty Horses* McCarthy's critics characteristically both wondered why the general reading public was oblivious to his work, and they constantly speculated about what circumstances would need to occur for this same public to discover his work. But after the fabulous commercial and critical success of *All the Pretty Horses* the questions about McCarthy and his career trajectory began to evolve. Would all those readers "new" to McCarthy continue with the final two volumes of "The Border Trilogy"—continue to read him, that is, whenever these later novels would perhaps dramatize cowboy characters riding into those darker recesses of the human condition that his earlier novels had so relentlessly explored? Conversely, would McCarthy's "new" readers turn to read these earlier novels whose forms, tone, deranged characters and disturbing subjects made them less accessible than *All the Pretty Horses*? With his public recognition seemingly at last secured, would two separate camps of McCarthy readers develop, those committed to the earlier Southern Gothic novels versus those who favored "The Border Trilogy" and its revisionist critique of the American West's classic mythology?

CAREER

> *I never had any doubts about my abilities. I knew I could write. I just had to figure out how to eat while doing this.*
> —CORMAC MCCARTHY

Charles McCarthy, Jr., was born on July 20, 1933, in Providence, Rhode Island, the eldest son and third oldest of six children born to

Charles Joseph and Gladys Christina McGrail McCarthy. Though named after his father, his name was legally changed early on (it is not clear at whose behest) to Cormac, Gaelic for "son of Charles" (the Irish chieftain Cormac McCarthy built Blarney Castle). When Cormac McCarthy was four years old he moved with his mother and siblings to the Knoxville, Tennessee, area, to join his father who worked as a legal counsel for the Tennessee Valley Authority. During the remainder of the Great Depression and the World War II years, McCarthy was raised and educated as a Roman Catholic in what was then and is now a predominantly Protestant area. He graduated from Catholic High School in Knoxville in the spring of 1951 and enrolled in the fall at the University of Tennessee for the 1951–52 school year, apparently declaring a liberal arts major upon his entrance. But he left the university in 1953 as the Korean War was winding down to serve a four-year stint in the U.S. Air Force. Two of his four years in the Air Force were spent in Alaska, where he hosted a radio show and began, apparently for the first time in his life, a regimen of serious reading.

After his discharge from the military in 1957, McCarthy returned to Knoxville and re-enrolled in the University of Tennessee, this time taking classes mostly in engineering and business administration. In his last two years at the university he published two stories (under the name "C. J. McCarthy, Jr.") in the literary supplement to the university's magazine *The Phoenix*: "Wake for Susan" (October 1959) and "A Drowning Incident" (March 1960). In both 1959 and 1960 he received the university's Ingram-Merrill Foundation grant for creative writing. Committed to the craft of his writing rather than to his academic study, he left Knoxville in 1961 without completing his bachelor's degree and moved with his first wife to Chicago, where he worked in an auto parts warehouse or as an auto mechanic while completing his first novel. Within a short period of time McCarthy and his wife and son returned to Tennessee, and after the dissolution of his first marriage McCarthy traveled around the South, living for a time in Asheville, North Carolina, and later in New Orleans's French Quarter. After completing the manuscript of his first novel, McCarthy sent the unsolicited work to Random House, where it eventually attracted the attention of Albert Erskine, long-time editor of Faulkner's fiction. In May 1965 Random House published McCarthy's first novel, *The Orchard Keeper*. In addition to receiving mostly favorable notices from mostly southern-based reviewers, *The Orchard Keeper*—whose character John Wesley in certain ways foreshadows John Grady Cole in *All the Pretty Horses*—received that year's William Faulkner Foundation Award for that year's "best" first novel by an American.

With the support of a $5,000 travel fellowship from the American Academy of Arts and Letters in 1965 and a two-year Rockefeller Foundation grant in 1966, McCarthy traveled to Europe, ostensibly to research his family's ancestry in preparation for his next novel. He settled on the island of Ibiza with his second wife, an English-woman who worked as a singer and dancer on the ocean liner that conveyed him across the Atlantic. On Ibiza he completed the revisions of *Outer Dark*, and in late 1967 the pair returned to Tennessee, living for a time in a small house on a pig farm near Rockford, just south of Knoxville. After the 1968 publication of *Outer Dark*, which featured an incestuous brother-sister relationship and their search for the abandoned child they produced, McCarthy received a Guggenheim Fellowship to work on his next novel, eventually titled *Child of God*. In the course of writing this novel, McCarthy was forced to take on various part-time jobs once the Guggenheim stipend expired. As his wife Anne DeLisle told McCarthy's interviewer from *The New York Times Magazine* in 1992, "someone would call up and offer him $2,000 to come speak at a university about his books. And he would tell them that everything he had to say was there on the page. So we would eat beans for another week." Simultaneously deploying and revising the "grotesque" tradition in Southern fiction, McCarthy's *Child of God* appeared finally in 1973. Based on the life of a serial killer and necrophiliac who ranged rural Tennessee's wooded hills and cohabited with his victims in caves, *Child of God* was alternately praised for its formal brilliance and seriously critiqued for its objective, non-judgmental treatment of its controversial subject matter and main character. Writing in the *New Yorker* magazine, Robert Coles predicted McCarthy's dark and complex subjects, as well as his resistance to contemporary intellectual and literary trends would determine his fate "to be relatively unknown and often misinterpreted."

Three years later, during the 1976 holiday season, McCarthy abruptly decided to leave Tennessee (and Anne DeLisle) and move to El Paso, Texas ("One of the last real cities left in America," he reportedly has said). At that time, McCarthy had developed a small, but loyal following among readers who basically christened him the true heir to the Southern Gothic fictional tradition exemplified by Faulkner and Flannery O'Connor. After January 1977, though, McCarthy's regular readers were now forced to wonder what the move to El Paso signified with regard to his future writing projects. Initially, little except McCarthy's zip code and status as a married man seemingly had changed. His first publication after the move to El Paso was *Suttree* (1979), a semi-autobiographical novel set in Knoxville that centered on a man who rejects his relatively privileged family and lives on a houseboat while carousing with other misfits and drunkards near the city's polluted river. Apparently a manuscript that had been in progress for two decades, *Suttree* was compared by some critics to such novels as James Joyce's *Portrait of the Artist as a Young Man*, not only because of the novel's seemingly autobiographical slant but also because of its formal experimentation with language and narrative point of view. Walter Sullivan wrote in the *Sewanee Review* that with the publication of *Suttree* McCarthy should be regarded as "the most talented novelist of his generation . . . the only writer to emerge since World War II who can bear comparison to Faulkner."

Yet with *Suttree* now finally completed, and with McCarthy now apparently committed to residing in the American Southwest—the direction Cornelius Suttree heads at novel's end—McCarthy's career began a different trajectory. "I've always been interested in the Southwest," he has said in the only interview he has granted to date. "There isn't a place in the world you can go where they don't know about cowboys and Indians and the myth of the West." "He always thought he would write the great American western," DeLisle has stated. With the support of a MacArthur Fellowship (the so-called "genius grant") awarded him in 1981, the nearly 50-year-old McCarthy quit living in motels or renting apartments, houses, or barns. He bought a small stucco house behind a shopping mall in El Paso, conducted extensive historical research and reading, and personally scouted—in various old pickup trucks he restored—the United States-Mexico borderland traversed in the late-1840s by a band of depraved mercenaries who killed Indians to sell their scalps to local authorities on each side of the border.

Four years after receiving the MacArthur Fellowship, McCarthy published the result of this historical research and personal travel under the title *Blood Meridian or the Evening Redness in the West* (1985). McCarthy's fifth novel depicted horrific scenes of violence which recalled the excesses of his earlier *Child of God*, incorporated a highly-allusive Shakespearean and Biblical rhetorical style, and portrayed an Ahab-like central character named Judge Holden. Critic Tom Pilkington neatly defined McCarthy's hybridized fusion of the historical romance, the Southern Gothic tradition, and the literary western to be "the illegitimate offspring of Zane Grey and Flannery O'Connor," whose "delivering physician" was the Marquis de Sade. Also compared by reviewers to Sam Peckinpah's violent western films and Hieronymus Bosch's hallucinatory art, *Blood Meridian* — though reportedly selling less than 2,000 hardback copies — developed a cult readership and solidified McCarthy's reputation as a "writer's writer." As it has turned out, *Blood Meridian* was the first of four novels McCarthy published between 1985 and 1998 that dramatized the historical transformation of the southwestern borderlands between the late 1840s setting of *Blood Meridian* and the late 1940s and early 1950s setting of "The Border Trilogy" inaugurated by *All the Pretty Horses*.

Over the next seven years, while a few academic critics began taking stock of his writing, McCarthy produced no new fiction. He continued to protect his anonymity. In fact, as reported by two of McCarthy's earliest and most-committed critics (Edwin T. Arnold and Dianne C. Luce), McCarthy was still so anonymous that the Arena Stage group in Washington, D.C., having decided in 1991 to produce his play *The Stonemason* (about an African-American stonemason and his family living in Louisville), "were surprised to discover that McCarthy was not a young black playwright." After his long-standing editor Albert Erskine retired from Random House, McCarthy moved over to Knopf publishers, one of Random House's subsidiary publishing arms. And for the first time in a career that was now three decades old, he acquired a literary agent.

In the fall of 1991 McCarthy delivered the completed manuscript of *All the Pretty Horses* to his editor at Knopf. His publisher arranged with *Esquire* magazine to print an excerpt from the novel the following March, and in late April 1992, just a couple of weeks prior to the novel's official release, McCarthy's interview with Richard Woodward appeared in *The New York Times Sunday Magazine*. Published on May 11th, 1992, and identified as the first volume of "The Border Trilogy," *All the Pretty Horses* entered the ranks of the *New York Times* hardback bestseller list a month later. In November the novel was named winner of the National Book Award for fiction, and by the year's end it had seemingly made every major American newspaper's and magazine's "best books of 1992" list. In early March 1993 the book was named winner of the National Book Critics Circle award for fiction and in April, when its hardback run ended, the novel had gone through twenty-two printings (for more on the book's sales and reception see chapters three and four). As the headline to one enthusiastic review of the novel trumpeted, "Finally! World Discovers Cormac McCarthy."

Throughout the rest of the decade the release of paperback editions and audio book productions, as well as the novel's publication by Picador in Great Britain, and the sporadic news of a Hollywood film production served to sustain readership interest. In 1994 McCarthy published the second volume in "The Border Trilogy," *The Crossing*, which centers on the adventures of a pair of brothers in southern New Mexico and Mexico. Devoted readers of McCarthy's trilogy awaited the promised 1996 publication of its final volume, *Cities of the Plain*, but this novel—which unites the two major figures from the trilogy's first two volumes—did not appear until 1998, the year production finally began on the film adaptation of *All the Pretty Horses*. Starring Matt Damon as John Grady Cole and Henry Thomas as Lacey Rawlins, director Billy Bob Thornton's two-hour film version of McCarthy's novel, edited from the uncut four-hour initial assemblage, was released to mixed reviews on Christmas Day 2000.

Meanwhile, McCarthy's continued efforts to safeguard his privacy—while not as fabled as those of his contemporary writer-peer Thomas Pynchon—spawned a new set of rumors about his future life and writing. Having completed the border trilogy, would McCarthy leave El Paso? Where would he decide to live? Has this writer, now nearing seventy years of age, exhausted his southwestern material? What will his next novel depict? As of this writing, Mc-

Carthy still lives in El Paso (though he has changed residences), has recently remarried, and is scheduled to deliver the manuscript of his next novel (rumored to be set in New Orleans and also involving an offshore drilling rig location in the Gulf of Mexico) to Knopf sometime during the late-spring or the summer of 2001.

OVERVIEW

> *There's no such thing as a life without bloodshed. I think the*
> *notion that the species can be improved in some way, that*
> *everyone could live in harmony is a really dangerous idea.*
> *Those who are afflicted with this notion are the first ones to*
> *give up their souls, their freedom. Your desire that it be that*
> *way will enslave you and make your life vacuous.*
> —CORMAC McCARTHY

Both the ranges of his subject matter and his evolving experiments with narrative forms make it difficult to generalize about McCarthy's body of work to date. From *The Orchard Keeper* to *Cities of the Plain*, McCarthy combines in differing proportions philosophical speculations, propulsive narrative sequences, inset stories, idiomatic dialogue scenes, and finely honed landscape descriptions to create the novels' overall "texture." With regard to his four southwestern novels alone, *Blood Meridian* presents more scenes of depraved violence, a greater range of stylistic registers, and more frequent metaphysical musings than does the border trilogy generally and *All the Pretty Horses* particularly. Moreover, its intense revision of the nineteenth-century historical romance form contrasts with the border trilogy's more measured use of literary conventions and imagery derived from the pastoral and quest romance traditions. With regard to "The Border Trilogy" volumes themselves, *All the*

Pretty Horses offers a more linear and sparer departure-return adventure plot, a more pivotal romance subplot, and fewer extended inset stories than can be found in *The Crossing*. And making any assessment of McCarthy's overall achievement even more difficult is the fact that sound arguments can be made on either side of the proposition that the themes, narrative forms, and prose style of McCarthy's four southwestern borderlands are continuous with those elements of his southern novels.

To be sure, the pervasive influence in the southern novels of Joyce's and Faulkner's narrative experiments with more than one point of view contrasts with the greater influence in the southwestern novels of Melville's metaphysical voice and Hemingway's more objectivist narrative and descriptive techniques. Nevertheless, regardless of their different settings, regional character types, and surface generic features (e.g., the popular western versus the Southern grotesque tradition), some important concerns remain constant throughout McCarthy's eight novels. His work thus may be said to illustrate the "truth" of what an older Mexican man tells Billy Parham in *The Crossing*: that because there is, finally, only one story to tell in this world—one ultimately involving violence and death—any and every storyteller has as his or her task not that of choosing "his tale from among the many that are possible. . . . The case is rather to make many of the one"(143).

The several variations on the "one" true tale elaborated by McCarthy's novels begin with the great fact of historical change as this is realized by conflicts between cultures or classes and within a family's generations. McCarthy's principal characters confront the demise of their established ways of life, occupations, and traditions—such as the end of the family cattle ranching operation in Texas detailed at the outset of *All the Pretty Horses*—and thus endure both physical and psychological dislocations. Either because of the forces set in motion by modernization or because of their own felt existential alienation, McCarthy's often-youthful characters fundamentally perceive, to use a line from *All the Pretty Horses*, that "there was something missing for the world to be right or he right in it" (23).

As a result of a felt absence in the world and human existence — figuratively rendered in the novels as the death of a relative or the dissolution of a family unit — the typical McCarthy protagonist is a social outcast or nomadic exile hoping to find that "something missing for the world to be right," which critic Vereen Bell translates as the desire "to be one with the earth and to live in genuine human communion." McCarthy portrays various quests to find this desired resonance with the natural and human worlds as processual journeys to find a lost child or a missing brother; to recover a stolen or lost horse; to rescue a whore from her pimp; or to return a wolf to her Mexican home range. McCarthy's "one" tale, then, braids together the themes of loss and exile, of inevitable social conflict and resultant human alienation, with the abiding theme of the journey or quest for an enlightened existence in, to cite a key word in *All the Pretty Horses*, one's true "country."

But during their migrations across various borders (national; cultural; psychological; class), McCarthy's characters typically discover four things. They come to understand the frightfully ephemeral nature of the world and its possessions. They come to see how this "waiting world" is not only indifferent to human needs and desires but also is simultaneously beautiful and horrific. They come to understand the constructed — hence provisional and contingent rather than absolute and universal — nature of human "truths" in this world. And through the impress of past events that always bear on present realities, they learn the hard way both about the constraints on human free will and that, as McCarthy states, "there is no such thing as a life without bloodshed." So McCarthy's characters strive, on the one hand, to order and control the world with their principles and beliefs; their tools, languages, systems, and maps; and their legal documents—and their disciplinary rituals and ceremonies that require, usually, the sacrifice of blood. But on the other hand, however much his characters desire secure foundations, their fate is rather to traverse a fluid, liminal landscape, usually blinded or confused precisely because their philosophical abstractions, their schemes, categorizations, and names, and their inherent prejudices and passions prevent them from truly seeing the world as it is, much less their place in it. Encountering "greed and foolishness and a love of blood" (239)—the "constant" of history according to Alfonsa in *All the Pretty Horses*—McCarthy's characters characteristically experience a chastening, if not tragic fall from innocence into experience.

McCarthy's fictional world is an implacable, ruthlessly determining world. In its various manifestations it remains a world "beyond reckoning," as Judge Holden claims in *Blood Meridian*, one governed—as far as anyone can tell—by death's haunting and calamitous presence, by the landscape's interlaced matrix of elements, and by humankind's hereditary instincts and desires that McCarthy repeatedly images as "blood." It is a fictive world that in every instance discloses McCarthy's indebtedness to those exemplary writers—Melville, Dostoyevsky, and Faulkner—who also have found it imperative, in McCarthy's words, to "deal with issues of life and death." It is a world whose apparent stress on the determining influence of both the physical environment and hereditary human instincts (sexual desire; violent aggression) extends the tradition of American literary naturalism exemplified by such writers as Jack London, Stephen Crane, Theodore Dreiser, Richard Wright, Ernest Hemingway, Dashiell Hammett, and Nathanael West. From this perspective, one virtue of McCarthy's fiction arises from its relentless stripping away of the illusory "truths" humans concoct to cover up the hard fact that the world existing between or beyond our acts and ceremonies or our dreams and realities offers no lasting solace and guarantees no progress.

Still, even as his orphaned characters' fates clearly trouble the myth of the American Adam who regenerates himself by fleeing society and "lighting out for the territory" in the manner of Huckleberry Finn, McCarthy's readers should consider a further point. Any "alien" world conceived as "ruthless in selecting" or "lying in wait," to use phrases from *All the Pretty Horses* and *The Crossing*, is, as McCarthy's participial grammar here suggests, a *performative* world. A performative world is one always being created as well as one already created. It is world in which, as the Judge says in *Blood Meridian* or as Perez tells John Grady Cole in the Saltillo prison, "anything is possible." One of McCarthy's stylistic signatures underlines the contingent "open" world that survives amidst the constraints closing down on human agency: when his narrator deploys a series of sentence fragments introduced by the subjunctive expression "as if," we see how each fragment offers a different explanatory perspective on whatever action or thought has initiated the sequence, thus troubling the notion that any one perspective can provide total knowledge. Regardless of history's brutality and the natural world's indifference, then, McCarthy's narrative voice does not finally promote nihilism, cynicism, despair — or a backward leap toward some incongruous faith in universal ideals or eternal truths.

As their stories proceed episodically to flesh out McCarthy's "one" true tale, his narrators dramatize how the arduous quest both to be in and witness the concrete here and now can lead at times to a revelatory moment. The revelation is that while all truths, values, beliefs, and things in the world are perishable, they are at the same time also potentially renewable. And with this awareness in mind, the primitive, yet vital pleasure of belonging *unconditionally* to the world as it is — not as a mirror of one's projections — is experienced and savored by McCarthy's characters. In the end, if not from the beginning, at the textured heart of McCarthy's fiction is the logic of the compelling "event." The "event" as an unexpected, and at times largely unfathomable encounter of humans and animals on the intersecting paths, streets, and roads in McCarthy's fictional landscapes functions to disrupt the Enlightenment tradition's rational, cognitive map of the world. The at-times horrific ruptures disclosing McCarthy's prevailing ethic of loss do not always overwhelm. They also occasionally metamorphose to produce a durable ethic of generosity — as when a gypsy stops to doctor a horse stabbed in *The Crossing* and tells a magical story about an airplane lost in the mountains; as when farmworkers in *All the Pretty Horses* give Cole a lift, their smiles and good will said to possess the "power to protect and to confer honor and to strengthen resolve and it had power to heal men and bring them to safety long after other resources were exhausted"(219).

The Novel

*He stood at the window of the empty cafe and watched the
activities in the square and he said that it was good that God
kept the truths of life from the young as they were starting out
or else they'd have no heart to start at all.*

(284)

INTRODUCTION: THEMES, STRUCTURE, NARRATIVE VOICE

All the Pretty Horses takes its title from a children's lullaby
that, in the manner of all lullabies, offers a contractual promise: if,
"little baby," you do not cry but instead go straightaway to sleep,
then "When you wake, / You shall have, / All the pretty horses—/
Blacks and bays, / Dapples and grays, / Coach and six-a little
horses." Near the beginning of the novel's final chapter, as John
Grady Cole stops for lunch and to rest his horse outside the Mexican village of La Vega, he relates the story of his adventures to some
children sitting beside him and sharing his sandwiches and fruit.
His narration of events to that point in the novel, however, discloses

anything but the fulfilled promises or the dreamy satisfaction of wishes and desires promised by lullabies:

He told them how they had come from another country, two young horsemen riding their horses, and that they had met with a third who had no money nor food to eat nor scarcely clothes to cover himself and that he had come to ride with them and share with them in all they had. This horseman was very young and he rode a wonderful horse but among his fears was the fear that God would kill him with lightning and because of this fear he lost his horse in the desert. He then told them what had happened concerning the horse and how they had taken the horse from the village of Encantada and he told how the boy had gone back to the village of Encantada and there had killed a man and that the police had come to the hacienda and arrested him and his friend and that the grand-mother had paid their fine and then forbidden the novia to see him anymore.

(243–44).

Now scenes of people eating and sharing stories while on the road or in a village's public spaces and restaurants are common in McCarthy's novels. But in this instance, Cole's synopsis basically presents the novel's overall trajectory of events during his 1950 adventure in Texas and Mexico. At this particular moment, in short, his narration provides an analogy for or epitome of the whole novel. What is the function and significance of this story that mirrors or re-duplicates the novel's larger story? As the rhythmic repetition of the past perfect verb forms ("had come," "had met," etc.) in this narrative suggests, the events enumerated in Cole's discourse have already occurred in his recent past—including the "grandmother's" pivotal speech act barring the young lovers from seeing each other. As a result, Cole's inset story doesn't particularly function to maintain or even advance the novel's action. However, because the residue of the "grandmother's" interdiction powerfully saturates the present moment of the storytelling, Cole's narrative synopsis does function in two other ways: 1) to offer an explanation for what has happened to this point in the novel; and 2) to clarify and reinforce both the novel's thematic vision and its basic structuring principle.

As is the case with the larger narrative within which it appears, Cole's inset story emerges as an episodic journey involving various encounters and conflicts with humans and animals. These encounters and conflicts provoke certain decisions that in turn produce grave consequences. As is also the case with the novel's overarching story, his compressed narrative thematically traverses a landscape dominated by desire. In this particular topography burning passion and primal violence transgress legal codes and collide with the culture and customs of "another country." As a result, like the novel's overall movement, Cole's saga thematically courses from community and possession to isolation and dispossession (the loss of family and friends, of horses, of a lover, of lives). So the utopian dream of mastery and control embedded in the lullaby's promise of one's possessing "all the pretty horses," represented by the first chapter's image of Cole and Lacey Rawlins stealing away under the cover of night with "ten thousand worlds for the choosing"(30)— this dream at this point near the novel's end has been dashed by Cole's somber recognition of all the forces—say a God who deals in lightning; say a grandmother who wheels and deals—opposing any mastery over the world and any satisfaction of one's heart's desire. So both the necessity and the heavy weight of some final reckoning come to haunt Cole's telling of his quest and his fall from innocence into experience, one which hits bottom with the emphatic falling rhythm of the final phrase "forbidden the novia to see him anymore."

In Chapter Three, during the fourth day of his and Cole's imprisonment at Saltillo, Rawlins tells Cole an even more condensed explanation of events: "All over a goddamned horse." To which summary statement Cole replies, "Horses had nothin to do with it" (185). When Cole relates his story to the children in the cottonwood grove outside La Vega in Chapter Four, though, he understands that while this matter of the *novia* remains crucial, this other matter of losing and recovering a "wonderful horse" is a significant element in the "all" of "it." All of these metafictional comments venture through narration an explanation for or interpretation of *the* larger story. Besides providing a method for developing characterization, their presence underlines McCarthy's great theme about the constructed—which is to say, personally and politically motivated—nature of all narrative discourse. This particular theme, furthermore, binds the novel's plotted action to the narrator and characters' more philosophical reflections about the meaning of human existence and about the difficult task of finding truth in the world. Reconstructing a true account of a horse's ownership or discovering through discourse the real motives and true nature of the relationship between three young American horsemen who have crossed the border both propels the plot forward and simultaneously represents an inquiry into the fundamental nature of truth and value.

McCarthy's thematic exploration of the "constructed" nature of both knowledge and narratives asks readers, by extension, to attend to the narrative voice's presence. Cole's and Rawlins's verbal exchange in the Saltillo prison appears in *direct* discourse form, as quoted dialogue promoting the illusion of "original" utterances in style as well as content. By contrast, Cole's narrative to the children of "all that had happened" appears in *indirect* discourse form, as the narrator's paraphrase of the content of Cole's tale. Put simply, whereas Cole tells about events McCarthy's narrator actually does the speaking at this moment. As this narrative performance develops, McCarthy's narrative voice distinctively foreshortens and simplifies Cole's recitation, primarily by deploying—through the regular repetitions of the conjunction "and"—a serial grammar whose coordination of elements (rather than subordination) cumulatively presents the sequential actions without distinction or hierarchy. Significantly, the narrator's indirect discourse also works to abstract or stylize the principal characters and the scene itself (the horsemen; "the wonderful horse"), while its presentation of events in successive verb clauses emphasize sheer motion and energy at the expense of the characters' motives or intentions. These features, along with the repetition of certain sounds and the relatively straightforward diction, promote the sense that a communal, rather than individualized, narrative voice is speaking.

The effects of McCarthy's indirect discourse are both local and general. Through the principles of repetition and contrast (from the act of joining and sharing to the act of separating and forbidding) Cole's inset story appears as a panoramic, highly composed assemblage. In this composed picture, the narrator's accumulating serial grammar, repetitious sounds, and refusal to psychologize combine to distance the story from the moment of its telling and thus to surround it with an air of mythic enchantment. More specifically, the actions and actors in this panoramic picture appear to be all *surface*. That is, the narrative voice's coordination of separate actions via the conjunctive splicing of "and" depicts the story's agents moving through or occupying an undifferentiated, foreground plane where the sunlight—and the lightning from God and men's firearms—falls equally on each element in the additive sequence. Through such stylistic maneuvers, McCarthy's narrative voice locates whatever available meaning there is (or can be attributed to) in the events described in the *local and present*—in what appears pragmatically visible before one's eyes or is felt rhythmically by the body either in the living or in the later remembering and telling of events.

The general point to make here, then, is that Cole's inset story not only reduplicates the novel's themes about the constructed nature of narratives, the constraints on human agency, and the quest motif. By stressing the local and present appearance of surfaces, the narrator's indirect discourse advances the idea of being-in-the-world as being completely present in each and every moment of its appearing in the here and now. What materializes before the human senses at bottom neither opposes nor veils profundity and reality. It rather evidences the very profundity of reality. By troubling the traditional philosophical oppositions of surface/depth or figure/ground, the narrator's indirect discourse signals the novel's strenuous critique of abstract, schematizing thought and the Enlightenment tradition's faith in rationality. As Don Hectór tells Cole in Chapter Two, "we don't believe that people can be improved in their character by reason"(146).

By way of introducing the novel's themes, style, and structure, another point remains to be made here. While discussing McCarthy's *Blood Meridian*, Denis Donoghue perceptively notes that McCarthy's largely episodic novels are basically indifferent to any plotting that would develop or complicate a story. As a result, McCarthy's fiction energetically presents incidents in simple succession, with little or no sense of their being pointed toward a climax or resolution. I have been making a similar point here about the narrator's indirect discursive rendering of Cole's storytelling to the children. Still, the careful reader will perhaps have already noticed that here — and for that matter elsewhere in *All the Pretty Horses* — the case is subtly different. For one thing, amidst all the compound sentences strung together by the "ands" a more discriminatory logic does in fact emerge in the narrator's indirect discourse. In the middle of the narrator's paraphrase of Cole's story, a subordinate clause informs us that the third young man who joins the first two horsemen from "another country" did in fact have a purpose: he "had come to ride with them and share in all they had." We further learn that it was precisely "because of his fear" of lightning that his "wonderful horse" became lost in the desert. In the end, the narrator's rendering of Cole's narrative performance discloses a causal logic that provisionally seeks to adjudicate events for purpose. In the process, it does in fact develop and point toward a complication, namely the grandmother's intervention in the lovers' affair and her prohibition against its continuance.

Now of course a complication such as this is by no means a resolution or climax—so perhaps the journey from *Blood Meridian* to *All the Pretty Horses* remains a short one after all. Maybe one fundamentally remains, as Cole's story seeks its own conclusion, captive to darker impulses, to cultural customs, to legal codes—and to an inscrutable natural world indifferent to human acts and dreams. Certainly McCarthy's narrative voice provides substantial evidence throughout the novel to support this conclusion. Even so, as this encounter with the gathered children suggests, McCarthy's narrative voice also portrays Cole getting some purchase on his experience precisely because he has paused on his journey and represents his experiences in narrative form. This portrayal occurs because the full meaning of Cole's experiences—much less the right way to proceed as a result of its complication—is *never* all that clear or fixed, even when pondered at the remove provided by narration.

The narrator's overall presentation of this narrative scene of instruction in Chapter Four—the detailing of the auditors present; the attribution of a cause and a purpose; the plot complication— reveals not only John Grady Cole's emergent maturity as a result of his adventures begun in the fall of 1949. It also confirms this narrative voice's greatly amplified sense of life. And it is this narrator's amplified sense that troubles the inset story's presiding notion that either a determining God or a determined grandmother possess the last word on matters. Precisely at this storied intersection where Cole's overriding personal tale of estrangement meets the more prescient narrative voice's mythopoetic gestures, the novel—as will

Cole in its remaining pages—takes its ethical stand, prepares to consume itself with the central questions implied here and dramatized throughout its length: How much suffering will and can a human endure? How much truth—what Alfonsa defines as the courage to see and accept "what is so"—will a human spirit dare confront in the arduous task of making a living in this alien world into which we're thrown?

CHAPTER ONE

They heard somewhere in that tenantless night a bell that tolled and ceased where no bell was and they rode out on the round dais of the earth which alone was dark and no light to it and which carried their figures and bore them up into the swarming stars so that they rode not under but among them and they rode at once jaunty and circumspect, like thieves newly loosed in that dark electric, like young thieves in a glowing orchard, loosely jacketed against the cold and ten thousand worlds for the choosing.

(30)

The longest of the novel's four chapters, Chapter One begins in mid-September 1949 at the Grady ranch near San Angelo, Texas, and concludes in early April 1950 when the teenage cowboys John Grady Cole and Lacey Rawlins arrive, after a long journey on horseback, at the La Purísima ranch in the Mexican state of Coahuila. The chapter is divided into fourteen unnumbered sections, eleven of which portray in quick succession Cole's loss of the family ranch, his estrangement from family and girlfriend, and his decision to head south in quest of some semblance of the pastoral life he has come to know and love while growing up on his maternal grandfather's ranch. After a short transitional scene describing the two boys' departure "like thieves newly loosed in that dark electric," two lengthy sections comprising two-thirds of the chapter's pages dramatize their month-long journey south into Mexico. Whereas in the chapter's first movement, Cole stands at sunset on the crest of a low rise "like a man come to the end of something"(5), at chapter's end, while he and Rawlins lie in the dark in the bunkhouse at La Purísima, he seemingly has reached the pastoral "paradise" described earlier to the pair on their journey across Coahuila's "cauterized terrain"(59; 57). The "end of something" signaled by the novel's opening image of Cole's dead grandfather lying in state ("That was not sleeping") evolves as the chapter proceeds into the image of the young cowboys as having magically transcended time and history: "This is how it was with the old waddies, aint it?" Rawlins says. "Yeah," Cole replies, and he then admonishes Rawlins to "[g]o to sleep" (96), his directive a veiled allusion to the promise in the lullaby that gives the novel its title.

The chapter's opening vignette announces its (and the novel's) central themes, plot, and imagery. In this initial scene a man enters a candlelit room to view the corpse of an older man, and after a few minutes leaves the room, venturing out on the dark and cold, windless prairie, where he stands with his hat in his hands and watches a train noisily approach and pass him in the false dawn. He then returns to the ranch house kitchen where he drinks coffee and converses in Spanish with the housekeeper, learning that the viewing room's candle had been lit by "La Senora" earlier in the night. The scene ends with the "just grainy light" of dawn appearing on the horizon and displacing its earlier images of candles and the train's headlamp. "La Senora" turns out to be young John Grady Cole's mother and the daughter of the dead man lying in state. Though her lighting a candle brings some light and warmth into the cold dark, her decision to sell the ranch to oil interests dispossesses her son, the family's eldest male heir, of his expected inheritance and provokes his journey south to Mexico. So in this vignette, the theme of transformation and loss, signaled by the death of a family patriarch, metamorphoses into the theme of alienation in a dysfunctional family. Not only must Cole discover his mother's movements through another source; he also recognizes that "La Senora" has been so removed from the family's life that she doesn't, in her earlier visit, re-arrange her dead father's hair so it looks like it did when he was alive.

McCarthy underscores this theme of transitional change accompanied by loss and alienation by introducing and then repeating several motifs and images throughout the chapter. In the first place, McCarthy underscores his vision of the world's ceaseless transitioning through time by situating key scenes either at transitional moments or in transitional spaces: sunrise and sunset moments, as well as dramatic changes in the weather, organize individual scenes and even structure whole chapters; threshold or borderland spaces (doorways and windows; mountain passes; the margins of watercourses) literally and metaphorically appear as characters negotiate their physical and psychological rites of passage. In the novel's opening scene McCarthy's narrator positions Cole on the cold prairie just before dawn, between the still, candlelit ranch house (the old pastoral West) and the moving, noisy train (the new industrial West) whose artificial light anticipates the coming dawn. Secondly, the image of the passing train with its brilliant headlamp concludes a leitmotif that can be defined as "the disturbance of an existing equilibrium as a result of some motion or event". The grandfather's death and the novel's opening image of the candle flame twisting and seeking to right itself in the drafty air are paralleled by the image of the train's motion making the ground shudder and its headlamp illuminating the barbed wire fence running parallel to the track.

These images actually perform double duty, for they further signal a third leitmotif McCarthy will develop throughout the novel's pages. This motif involves reflections — produced by glass and water surfaces—and cast shadows. In the opening scene, not only the candle flame but also its reflected image in the pierglass is said to twist and right itself in the air. Moreover, our first view of Cole is actually the image of his standing black-suited figure reflected in a "waisted cutglass vase." Like "the portraits of forebears only dimly known to him all framed in glass and dimly lit above the narrow wainscotting" in the hallway behind him (3), Cole is initially framed by reflecting glass. As the chapter's first movement in San Angelo ends, however, Cole's farewell to his ex-girlfriend on the streets of San Angelo is described as his having "stepped out of the glass [of the Federal Building's windows] forever"(29). The variation in this imagistic motif of reflection confirms his intention to escape the framing narratives of his future being constructed by various adults.

Besides providing another method of characterization, the motifs involving both light imagery and reflections or shadows help unify disparate events in Chapter One and deepen the resonance of the chapter's familiar preparation-and-departure structure. Through the particular motif involving reflected images, moreover, McCarthy introduces another key theme besides those focusing either on historical change and transformation or on youthful alienation from parental authority. Nights in San Angelo sometimes find Cole outside his father's hotel, staring up at "where his father's shape or father's shadow would pass behind the gauzy window curtains." Later, after sighting from the crest of a Mexican mountain ridge "the country of which they'd been told," the young cowboys "could see like a reflection of their own fire in a dark lake the fire of the vaqueros five miles away" (15; 93). As the dreams and comments about horses in Chapter Two will also illustrate, these leitmotifs involving reflections and shadows and light imagery convey the novel's twofold thematic exploration of the human fall from community, harmony, and unity into isolation, division, and duality and the resulting human problem of adjudicating between appearances and reality in order to establish truth and value.

Before the train appears "like a ribald satellite of the coming sun"—another "double" image—Cole stands outside on the cold prairie "like some supplicant to the darkness over them all"(3). As chapter one's first movement in San Angelo proceeds, this youthful supplicant will entreat his father to intercede on his behalf, will seek the advice of a lawyer, will plead with his mother to lease him the ranch, and will ask Rawlins to join him on his intended journey to Mexico. Besides forecasting the novel's action, the image of Cole as a supplicant seeking for answers and some solace in the midst of dramatic changes in his "country" discloses how McCarthy endows the chapter's predominant journey structure with aspects of the mythic quest. The ghost Comanche nation that haunts the faint track Cole rides through the ranch's westernmost portion at sunset is said to bear "like a grail the sum of their secular and transitory and violent lives"(5). "We're like the Comanches was two hundred years ago," says Cole's cowboy-gambler father, now dying of cancer and still borne down by his brutal POW experience in World War II. "We dont know what's goin to show up here come daylight. We dont even know what color they'll be"(26). Though his comment obliquely refers to the intensified Cold War anxieties in 1949 caused by events in Mao's Red China, Cole's father's identification with the Comanche links the chapter's overarching theme of the American West's historical transformation to its quest and grail imagery. Elsewhere in Chapter One Cole journeys through a snowstorm to San Antonio hoping to find an answer in his mother's stage performance for "the way the world was or was becoming"(21). No prophetic answer materializes, and Cole the supplicant unsurprisingly will continue his quest. As the narrator says, even if he were "begot by malice or mischance into some queer land where horses never were," Cole "would have set forth to wander" until he had found that "something missing for the world to be right or he right in it"(23).

As Chapters Two and Four particularly reveal, for Cole this "something" necessary for "right" dwelling in the world has everything to do with horses and their instinctual way of being in the world. In Chapter One, however, the open range is mostly fenced, plagued by bad weather, marked by the detritus of an industrial civilization, and seemingly overrun with the cars of oil field scouts. It is, in short, an increasingly "queer land," this country that Cole can no longer claim as his own. So Cole's seeking takes him and Rawlins — and eventually the "gunsel" Jimmy Blevins — across the border and deep into Mexico during the chapter's long second movement. As Gail Morrison has suggested, McCarthy's plotting of the novel's linear journey south into Mexico is actually more complexly involved than it might seem to be at first glance. To take two examples: the chapter's first movement ends with Cole saying goodbye to his ex-girlfriend Mary Catherine, while its second movement ends with him gazing at Alejandra Rocha riding her gaited Arabian horse; the freak snowstorm during Cole's journey to San Antonio is paralleled by the thunderstorm and lightning that precipitates their eventual action to retrieve Blevins's horse at Encantada.

In Chapter One, furthermore, as the young cowboys search for that "paradise" described to them on the yonder side of the Sierra del Carmen (55), their journey progressively becomes more elemental, the increasingly more "alien"(52) humans and topography they encounter incrementally forcing an encounter with life's starker realities. Stripping off their clothes to cross the Rio Grande as if they were being baptized into a new life, the adventurers cross dry scrublands, pass through a barren windgap in the mountains, and then enter grasslands, which almost immediately give way to a forbidding desert terrain. As they travel south the sounds and sights of domesticated animals gives way to their hearing or talking about coyotes, wolves, and mountain lion attacks. Their eating in restaurants or buying canned goods evolves into their hunting and eating rabbit and deer. Their enjoyment of a Mexican family's hospitality early on in their journey evolves into their successive encounters with the "wild and strange" *zacateros*, the migrant traders, and the encamped waxmakers, one of whom sexually desires Blevins and offers Cole money for him. The chittering birds Cole hears in the brush during his sunset ride on the old Comanche trail evolves in the chapter's second movement into the birds dead and impaled on the spikes of a shrub in the aftermath of the pivotal, plot-changing thunderstorm in which Blevins loses his horse, clothes, and gun.

As is the case with the novel's other chapters, McCarthy endows Chapter One's developing adventure plot with greater resonance as a result of intratextual motifs, parallel (and inverted) dramatic structures, and repetitions of imagery and dialogue. But the main thing is that McCarthy's deceptively complex plotting of Cole's linear adventure south brings into greater relief his character and its initiatory rite of passage into mature adulthood. In Chapter One we understand—primarily through the dramatic foils provided by his father, Rawlins, and Blevins—that Cole is stubborn and rebellious, clearly ambitious, somewhat intolerant and impatient, and passionately idealistic. Like his grandfather—who refused to believe his son-in-law was killed in the war until he received dog tags to bury; who would fight any man who slandered his daughter (Cole's mother)—Cole is "ardenthearted"(6). Where Rawlins utters cliched pronouncements and rides an emotional roller coaster as their journey proceeds, Cole is more stoical and, like the vaqueros depicted at La Purísima at chapter's end, is "scornful of any least suggestion of knowing anything not learned at first hand"(96). Whereas Rawlins realistically forecasts bad things happening because of their riding with the impulsive and violent Blevins, and whereas he finally urges them to abandon Blevins, Cole twice refuses to abandon the thirteen-year-old boy to his fate. To the Rawlins who has earlier claimed that the mundane act of someone sneezing "in Arkansas or some damn place" could lead to "wars and ruination and all hell" (92), Cole naively says that their helping Blevins get his horse and gear back surely wouldn't cause them any undue trouble.

Cole's sentimental idealism underpins his charismatic presence and defines his naivete, his innocence as well as his immaturity. It also defines his capacity for self-deception. He refuses to accept that his father's divorce, terminal illness, and harsh experiences as a POW in World War II have changed the man where it counts, on the "inside," and in contrast to his father, whose view of the landscape is "made suspect by what he'd seen of it elsewhere" (23), the "ardenthearted" Cole rides on, in search of answers to be sure, but also in the belief that there are "ten thousand worlds for the choosing." On the eve of their fateful encounter with the horse thieves of Encantada, Cole recognizes that Rawlins was "right in all he'd said" [about taking their final chance to leave Blevins to his fate] — but "there was no help for it"(81). Rawlins said he was pretty sure what Cole's response would be to his plea to abandon Blevins before "somethin bad" happens (77). Cole, though, responds that he didn't know in advance of his saying it what his decision would be. His response thus accords with his earlier revelatory comment that on journeys one can't tell what's in a country "till you're down there in it"(59). Cole clearly has a rough and ready sense of honor, loyalty, and courage modeled after his grandfather's example — and as a man of action he is certain that "talk" is *not* everything. But he and his code of honor remain a work in progress, both being tried out and tested "down there in it," this "alien" country where Cole often is posed, to use a key McCarthy verb, "studying" things and people, increasingly uncertain and troubled about what it all might mean.

CHAPTER TWO

The old man shaped his mouth how to answer. Finally he said that among men there was no such communion as among horses and the notion that men can be understood at all was probably an illusion.

(111)

While looking out over the country where the sun "lay blood red among the shelving clouds" not long after they have crossed over the border, Rawlins asks Cole: "Where do you reckon that paradise is at?"(59) As Chapter One draws to a close, at still another sunset moment atop another mountain ridge, the pair finally glimpse "below them the country of which they'd been told": waterfowl fly before "the deep red galleries under the cloudbanks" off in the distance and, in the foreground, vaqueros drive cattle across deep grasslands "through a gauze of golden dust"(93). Bordered by mountains to the west and surrounded by desert on every other side, the fabled 27,500 acre La Purísima ranch, holding about 1,000 head of cattle and hundreds of wild horses, constitutes a sweetly-perfumed pastoral Eden of lush grass and plentiful and varied water supplies. Hired on by the ranch's foreman after interviewing them in his kitchen, Cole and Rawlins walk out into the darkness "where the moon was rising and the cattle were calling and the yellow squares of windowlight gave warmth and shape to an alien world"(95). The novel's opening image of feeble candle light and a dead man's yellowed moustache transformed now into the image of warm yellow light warding off an "alien world," La Purísima seemingly offers the young cowboys both sanctuary from their recent troubles at Encantada and an opportunity to sustain their dream of cattle ranching in the manner of Cole's grandfather.

In the novel's opening scene Cole presses his thumbprint in the candle wax pooling on a piece of oak furniture near his grandfather's corpse. As the brief pastoral interlude in Chapter Two develops—the chapter is only 54 pages long—Cole opportunistically puts his signature on the landscape in and around La Purísima, that territory depicted as a white blank space on the maps the young cowboys carry with them. With the previous chapter's subplot involving Blevins and his stolen bay horse relegated to the margins in Chapter Two, McCarthy further develops the main plot of Cole's coming-of-age through a series of tests and challenges which tempt body and soul.

Two other features highlight chapter two's presentation of Cole's developmental transition into manhood: the scenes involving Cole's interactions with and thoughts or dreams about horses; the scenes where various adults mentor Cole about "the truths of life"(284). After its opening scenes establish Cole's skills with and special knowledge of horses, the chapter dramatizes a doomed romance subplot involving Cole's affair with Alejandra Rocha, seventeen-year-old daughter of the ranch's wealthy and powerful owner Don Hectór Rocha. Cole's performance breaking, with Rawlins's assistance, sixteen wild horses in four days, leads to his elevated status as Don Hectór's chief assistant for the ranch's quarterhorse breeding program. "It's a opportunity for you," Rawlins initially admits when Cole moves his gear from the bunkhouse to the barn where he will work the mares and the ranch's imported black stallion (116). But when conversing a few nights later with Cole on a mesa during a rainstorm, Rawlins shrewdly ascertains that Cole—dispossessed of his grandfather's ranch in west Texas and unable himself to buy land in Mexico—has "eyes for the spread" as well as for Rocha's daughter (138).

Several obstacles block Cole's path to courtship and marriage of Alejandra Rocha. Though they are contemporaries who share similarly defiant, passionate temperaments, there are differences of class and national origin to consider. There are courtship customs and rituals that, in Mexico at least, must be respected. And, as it turns out, there is Cole's own duplicity and denial — revealed through a series of conversations he has with Don Hector and Alejandra's great aunt Alfonsa — with regard to the motives for his journey south and his involvement in "the affair at Encantada," the news of which has preceded his and Rawlins's arrival at the ranch. Lies beget greater lies (about why the stallion needs to be exercised; about who rides the stallion), and Alfonsa's warning that he should respect Alejandra's honor and leave off courting her fosters on Cole's part a disingenuous ambiguity. Quizzed by Rawlins about what Alfonsa had asked him to do, Cole says "I aint sure"; quizzed about whether he gave her his "word," Cole answers "I dont know if I did or not"(139).

The couple's sexual passion begets compromises and betrayal and, as the chapter ends, a vengeful father hunts with his greyhounds for Cole on the mountain, embodying in his action the answer to Rawlins's question to Cole on their first night at La Purísima: "You reckon they think we're on the run down here?"(96) But instead of killing Cole he calls in the Mexican police searching for the gringos who were accomplices of Blevins at Encantada, and the would-be American Adam and his comrade are expelled from the Mexican "Big Rock Candy Mountain"(55). Though appearing to be a sheltered pastoral enclave outside of time and history, La Purísima and its inhabitants in reality attest to the inescapable impact of human history's wheeling changes and bloody ruptures. Imagistically speaking, then, the rather benign thumbprint in candle wax at the novel's outset evolves into the "sutures" on the landscape made by fences and rails and paths, which transform into the "scars" — in Chapter Two, on Cole's cheek; on Alfonsa's left hand — that in Alfonsa's words "have the strange power to remind us that our past is real"(135).

Because the narrative voice typically does not either directly judge the action or portray his characters' interior lives, readers need to attend to McCarthy's repetition-with-variation method to sort out the novel's normative beliefs and values and to understand the stages of Cole's maturational development. As is the case with watching any stage drama or film, McCarthy's cinematically-styled novels demand readers notice, say, a dialogue sequence's unstated cues to decipher what is happening and what it might mean about theme or character development. When Rawlins charges Cole with having "eyes for the spread," for instance, Cole's response that he hadn't thought about it is belied by his looking at and then away from Rawlins toward the campfire in response to the latter's "Sure you aint." Readers need also to consider how the narrative voice's perspective — though at times closely identified with Cole's predicaments and consciousness — is nevertheless *not* always identical with that of the novel's major protagonists. Readers who complain that McCarthy's narrator overwhelms his adolescent characters with adult philosophizing and abstruse language miss the fundamental point that narrative disjunctures between Cole's character and the narrative voice's more expansive vision diagnose Cole's developmental progression. Indeed, largely because the narrative voice carves out space "betwixt and between" Cole and the reader, *All the Pretty Horses* essentially dramatizes a *critique* rather than a confirmation of the human desire for power and the rationalized language of mastery and control associated with the popular western novel or film.

McCarthy installs greater thematic coherence in the midst of the chapter's circular arrival-and-departure-at-daybreak structure through a motif involving the activity of hands and through repetitive images of burning things (wood; stars; lightning; eyes; passions), blood and hearts, paleness, water, and the colors blue and black. Early in the chapter, for example, Cole camps in the mountain overlooking the ranch, and, as his campfire burns down to coals, he lies on his back and gazes at the stars. He then places his hands at his sides and presses them "against the earth and in that coldly burning canopy of black he slowly turned dead center to the world, all of it taut and trembling and moving enormous and alive under his hands." "What's her name?" Rawlins asks him out of the darkness, clarifying what the narrator doesn't spell out, that for Cole the "all of it" imagined to be moving under his hands includes Alejandra Rocha (119), who in the chapter is frequently linked with heated motion and the colors blue and black As a young southwestern knight-errant questing for answers "about the way the world was or was becoming," Cole is at times gentle — as when he strokes and cups his hands to cover the wild horses' eyes while talking to them.

Yet he also imagines wild horses on the mesa "who knew nothing of him or his life yet in whose souls he would come to reside forever"; and he thinks about his voice eventually running through their brains "like the voice of some god come to inhabit them"(105). These hands gripping the earth by the campfire also grasp the mane of the black stallion that, like a god, he talks to in "biblical" phrases and that he rides immediately after it covers the mares in season, his "wildness within" identifying with the stallion's strength and sexual potency. These are the hands that cup themselves to lift the blue-eyed Alejandra onto a black horse and that eventually reach toward her nude body that — like the earth and like the corralled wild horses — "trembles" upon entering the laguna's warm black water and which will tremble and move under Cole's touch, that body whose pale skin paradoxically burns cold like the moon or "[l]ike foxfire in a darkened wood"(141). Whether turning wild animals into saddlehorses or riding the black stallion or loving Alejandra — all bodies imaged, like the earth he turns "dead center" to, as taut, trembling, and moving — thus discloses the "ardenthearted" Cole's grandiose, possessive desire for mastery and control.

After learning from Don Hectór about the plan to send Alejandra to France, Cole tells the vaquero Antonio that "he intended to know her heart" with regard to her feelings about him (147). Intending to know one's deepest intentions and desires is comparable to knowing what one "aims to do," to cite the question Cole keeps hearing in the wake of his grandfather's death and the impending sale of the ranch. By declaring his intention to know Alejandra's heart, Cole on the one hand reveals his newfound seriousness of purpose as well as his stubborn, idealistic faith that the various obstacles to their love can be surmounted. But on the other hand his declaration also reveals his inability or unwillingness to understand a crucial point made to him in Chapter Two. When Cole and Rawlins camp on the mountain to capture wild mares, the old *mozo* Luis talks to them about the souls of horses and men. Luis makes two claims highly relevant to our understanding both Cole's character development and the novel's ongoing critique of the desire to dominate through aggressive passion or the language of reason. Luis's first claim is that "the souls of horses mirror the souls of men more closely than men suppose." His second claim, though, is that "among men there was no such communion as among horses and the notion that men can be understood at all was probably an illusion"(111).

Throughout the novel wild horses represent an elemental, instinctual life force or principle of unbound, fluid energy. Through image repetitions and his characters' spoken thoughts and imagined dreams, McCarthy associates horses and their souls with the seamless world that exists before or in spite of the "cuts" made into it by abstract thinking and rational intellection and language, whose names, categories, labels, concepts, and schemes thus always mediate human interactions with the world. To borrow phrasing from the New Testament's *Corinthians I*, horses are believed to see the world face to face, not through a glass darkly—which becomes the human mode of apprehending the world. In Chapter One, the narrator's description of that "something" Cole would seek "for the world to be right or he right in it" is linked to the existence of horses. As the multiple connotations of the word "right" suggest, horses realize the utopian desire to exist in accordance with a just and genuine, not a counterfeit or false, world. For Cole, who dreams of some momentary collusion with the horse's authentic being, living in the presence of horses potentially offers atonement (at-one-ment), corroborating evidence of the world's overall harmony and sacred order—what his dream in Chapter Three depicts as a collective, musical "resonance"(162).

But, of course, as Cole tells Rawlins, "I aint a horse"(106). Mirroring Luis's claim about the lack of communion among men, Antonio finally tells Cole that no one can advise him about the desires of the heart. As the romance subplot develops, Chapter Two underlines Cole's existential isolation by physically separating him from Rawlins throughout most of the chapter and by depicting him lying awake at night, contemplating the vast cosmos into which sparks from his campfire float. Ironically, in the aftermath of Cole's performance as a horsebreaker the trussed-up horses whinny to one another "as if some one among their number were missing, or some thing"(107). The narrator's repetition of the word "missing" and the phrase "some thing" indirectly links the corralled horses' fate to the earlier description of Cole's seeking throughout some "queer land" for that "thing" or "something" that would make the world "right." This parallel linkage suggests the truth of Luis's initial claim about the souls of horses and men closely mirroring each other. However, the repetition of both cadence and phrasing in the two passages more cogently testifies to the truth of Luis's second claim: that it is an illusion to think men can be understood at all.

Given Cole's resolute determination, his compelling energy and demonstrable skill at his work, as well as his experiences with adults back in Texas, it is entirely understandable why he resists the advice of Don Hectór and Alfonsa and ignores their cautions and pointed warnings about who has "the power to say" what is and what will be in this different country. Nevertheless, a problem arises if readers either uncritically identify with Cole's character and his plight or believe the novel, through Cole's characterization, uncritically idealizes some macho masculine code. This is where recognizing the space carved out by the narrative voice betwixt and between Cole's character and the reader becomes an important consideration. Take, for instance, that lyric moment when Cole sees in the distance Alejandra's shrouded figure on horseback being caught by the wind and rain "in that wild summer landscape" of mountain, hills, and grassy plains. The narrator ends Cole's vision with this summary judgment: "real horse, real rider, real land and sky and yet a dream withal"(132). Connoting "despite that" or "nevertheless," the narrator's judgmental "yet" and "withal" succinctly differentiate those who can, like the narrator who speaks, recognize the dynamic interplay of dreams and reality from those who, like Cole at this moment, project a dreamscape despite the insistent presence of the "real." In direct contrast to Blevins's fear of lightning, Alejandra rides on "all seemingly unaware," even as lightning flashes from the black clouds piled up behind her. The Cole who projects "a dream withal" is similarly unaware of looming danger, so the narrator's dream reference reinforces how Cole's dreams and desires blind him to the "real," and cause him to sleepwalk through his days.

Like a pointillist painter, McCarthy throughout the chapter portrays the defiantly passionate Alejandra with splotches of blue, black, and pale hues—just like the weather and the land in this scene. For the reader who recalls how the thunderstorm in Chapter One acts as an agent in the plot, McCarthy's linkage here of landscape, weather, and character portends the violent consequences of the

couple's electric passion and complicates the chapter's marshalling
of images to connote Alejandra's virginal purity (pale like a chrysalis; white waterlilies). Simultaneously specifying something distinctive and something limited about Cole's cognitive projection of the
world, then, the novel's narrative voice here and throughout chapter
occupies a space both within and beyond or outside of Cole's
character. By recognizing such cues, by tracking the chapter's motif
of hands, and by understanding how the discourse on horses sugges-
tively distinguishes the truths of nature from humanity's constructed
truths, the reader should see beyond or through Cole's self-
aggrandizing vision and register how his passionate ambition and
naivete lead to a string of deceptions and evasions which compromise his integrity and blind him to the constraints of the "real."
Though he grandiosely imagines himself turning "dead center" to
the moving world when placing his hands on it, the fact remains —
as the chapter's related imagery of shrouds, gauze, and hoods suggests — that Cole still must learn how to see "what is so" as well as
what is "right," and to accept rather than deny responsibility for his
decisions and actions. In the meantime, as the chapter concludes,
instead of the world being centered by his shaping hands, Cole's
hands are cuffed by the Mexican police and he, along with Rawlins,
is led at daybreak away from the illusory paradise of La Purísima.

CHAPTER THREE

He half wondered if he were not dead and in his despair he felt well up in
him a surge of sorrow like a child beginning to cry but it brought with it
such pain that he stopped it cold and began at once his new life and the
living of it breath to breath.

(203)

Comprised of three long sections, Chapter Three details events in the seven week period between Cole's and Rawlins's forced departure from La Purísima and the beginning of Cole's solitary journey from Saltillo back to the ranch in order to speak with Alejandra and reclaim their horses Redbo and Junior. Within this overarching circular structure of departure and return, the chapter centers on the young Americans' initial imprisonment in Encantada and, later on, in the prison at Saltillo. Like the novel's other chapters, this chapter's journeys and events structurally cohere because of McCarthy's repetition and parallelism of scenes, motifs, and imagery. In this chapter, for instance, the boys' interviews with Perez and Cole's killing of the hired *cuchillero* in the Saltillo prison section mirror the scenes of the boys' interrogation by the Mexican captain and Blevins's murder in the earlier Encantada section. The money that Blevins pulls from his boot and thrusts at Cole as the Mexican captain leads him away to his death establishes a motif repeated in the chapter's Saltillo prison purgatory section when Alfonsa eventually sends money to arrange for Cole's and Rawlins's release.

Though clearly providing greater coherence for the novel's accumulating events, McCarthy's various repetitions also disclose subtle differences, inversions, or contrasts. These variances both contribute to the plot's forward momentum and highlight its theme and character development. Consider the above motif that could be labeled "the unexpected gift of money occasioned by a sacrifice" (Blevins's death; Alejandra's promise). In its first incarnation Blevins loses his boot while retrieving his cache of money, and the Mexican captain — ironically described as placing his hand at Blevins's back as if he were a kindly protector — escorts the boy across a clearing toward a grove of ebony trees. When Alfonsa's ransom arrangement materializes, the motif is re-introduced as Perez's man lifts the wounded Cole — his boots filled with blood — from the prison's open yard and delivers him to safety just as its lights come on and its horn sounds. On one level, that Cole has used Blevins's money covertly to buy a switchblade after Rawlins is knifed in the prison yard binds these disparate scenes together. Cole's killing of the *cuchillero* in self-defense thus suggests that a compensatory justice results from a balanced expenditure or an equal exchange of life and death.

Besides the obvious fact of the two Americans' contrasting fates, however, whereas Blevins is guided by his assassin's hands toward his death, Cole gets lifted like a child from the prison yard's darkness and is delivered safely to a lighted room. Along with propelling the plot forward, the motif's repetition with variation underlines how Chapter Three's depiction of the boys' descent into a hellish underworld of violence and depravity—one only hinted at in the earlier scene when one of the candlemakers offers to buy the half-naked Blevins—modulates images of darkness and death with images of rebirth and re-emergence. As the above epigraph reveals, the key moment in Cole's passage through purgatory occurs when he wonders, while recovering from his knife wounds in a stone room's womb-like darkness, if he were not already dead, feels a surge of sorrow "like a child beginning to cry," stifles this surge because of his bodily pain, and then begins "at once his new life and the living of it breath to breath."

At the chapter's outset the manacled Cole and Rawlins eat cold beans and tortillas cradled by a newspaper from Monclova as they travel with their armed police escort. The charges eventually levied against them by the Mexican captain at Encantada have been foreshadowed not only by specific events but also by the earlier chapters' imagery. Besides Rawlins's worry that associating with Blevins would get them "throwed in the jailhouse"(41), he and Cole playfully call each other "desperado" or facetiously identify themselves as "bandoleros." The novel's second image of Cole and Rawlins together is of the pair "spreadeagled on the blacktop like captives waiting some trial at dawn"(26). The narrator also associates key events with images of larceny or thievery: leaving Rawlins's place just before dawn, the boys are likened to "thieves in a glowing orchard"; Cole's first sexual liaison with Alejandra is said to be "sweeter for the larceny of time and flesh"(30; 140). Significantly, when the young American trio cross the Rio Grande, the narrator portrays them as "making for the alien shore like marauders"(45)m)—an image which foreshadows both Don Héctor's and the Mexican captain's interpretation of their motives for leaving Texas. As Chapter Three ends, however, McCarthy reworks the opening scene's reference to the Monclova newspaper. Beginning his return journey from Saltillo to La Purísima aboard a flatbed truck, Cole places his outstretched hands on the truck cab's roof to help balance himself, looking as a result "[a]s if he were some personage bearing news for the countryside. As if he were some newfound evangelical being conveyed down out of the mountains and north across the flat bleak landscape toward Monclova" (217).

An argument can be made that the combination of such imagery and foreshadowing, Rawlins's earlier intuition that Cole had "eyes for the spread," and the events of Chapter Three basically discloses the novel's latent investment in the formulaic popular western's ideology of American "progress" through violent conquest and dispossession of evil, nonwhite "Others" (the Mexican captain; the *cuchillero*). From this perspective, the chapter's concluding image of Cole as a "personage bearing news for the countryside" in the manner of a "newfound evangelical" seemingly stresses Cole's constant, unregenerate Adamic rebellion against authority, his supreme unwillingness to acknowledge limitations on his authority and power. Cole's resurrected appearance as a "newfound evangelical" could be said, then, to reinforce the Chapter Two image of Cole as a demigod who recites in biblical phrases "the strictures of a yet untabled law" testifying to his power and authority over all the mares and the black stallion he rides (128). From this perspective, McCarthy's particular imagery, foreshadowing, and plotting confirm Cole's resilient, but essentially static character, one whose task is to sustain his youthful idealism during his initiation into the world's "greed and foolishness and a love of blood," to cite Alfonsa's definition of the "constant in history"(239). Cole's killing of the *cuchillero*, defeat of the Mexican captain, and retrieval of their horses from Encantada, then, illustrates how the novel's sophisticated deployment of the formula western's iconography, character types, and themes ultimately celebrates rather than critiques the dominant culture's cowboy mythology.

Though raising important questions, this analytical perspective — like Perez's notion of the Anglo mind's typical "picture of the world"(192) — is finally "incomplete" and reductive of the novel's complexity. With regard to the Chapter Three's final image, for instance, it is important to recognize that the narrator, not Cole, describes Cole's appearance via the two "as if" clauses bearing religious connotations. As is the case with sexual passion exploding at a ranch named after the Immaculate Conception or when Cole in Chapter Four watches a wedding procession in the rain, the slight disjunction here between character and narrator establishes a quiet irony. From a distance Cole may *appear* as if he were a "newfound evangelical." But the *reality* is that his scarred body has just emerged from a place where God is said not to exist and where men are judged not by the Gospel's message of peace, love, and mercy but rather by their bedrock "readiness to kill"(182).

However slight, the gap between appearance and reality permits the passage's ironizing perspective to emerge, and doubt about the "fit" between Cole's character and the overlaid religious imagery brings two points into view. First, the reference to the "news" and "newfound" culminate the chapter's latent stress on rebirth imagery.

At the end of Chapter Three Cole does importantly emerge as
"newfound." Following on Cole's sense that he has begun a "new
life" while recovering from his knife wounds, "newfound" draws
together at chapter's end the successive scenes depicting Cole moving from darkness into areas of light, awakening from dream-laden
sleep, emerging from the pale chrysalis of a shift or the bandages
covering his body, and standing in the soft morning rain in new
clothes. Secondly, though he undoubtedly does not appear or sound
as forlorn as Rawlins does, Cole is hardly an unrepentant idealist or
an "important personage" bearing, like an "evangelical," tidings of
a redemptive future. To be sure, like an "evangelical" whose dissem-
ination of the Gospels' teachings may well conflict with established
ecclesiastical authority, Cole's defiance of cultural conventions and
parental authority means he will seek a face-to-face meeting with
Alejandra to verify his suspicion about the terms Alfonsa arranged
for his release. Still, if Cole plausibly can be said to bear any "news"
for the countryside, that news — after his having witnessed and participated in the violent deaths of other men — would have little to
do with redemption through faith and grace. Like the ghost nation
of Comanche "bearing" as they ride "like a grail the sum of their
secular and transitory and violent lives," Cole has not only witnessed
but also participated in sacrificial violence, has been fully initiated
into the human condition of being "pledged in blood and redeemable in blood only"(5).

In concert with the novel's overall play with the imagery of
appearance and reality, the "newfound evangelical" image also underscores the novel's theme about the necessity for humans to see
the world as it is instead of as a projection of what one desires it to
be. As Cole's passage through the prison's purgatory stresses, this
task entails having the courage to recognize and negotiate the
world's evil which, as Perez tells Cole, materially "goes about on its
own legs" and inevitably "will come to visit" everyone "some

day"(195). The narrator's ironic applique of religious salvation imagery to a sixteen-year-old cowboy further reinforces the novel's theme of human division or alienation from, as described in Cole's dream about becoming one of the running wild horses, that "resonance which is the world itself and which cannot be spoken but only praised"(162). Having the courage to see the world as it is and, in the process, negotiate its evil also means having the courage to jettison any established values, beliefs, and meanings which—like the shadow cast on the wall by the iron grid over the judas-hole of the Encantada jail's wooden door—render the world "out of true"(161). Instead of the certitude of belief typically associated with a "newfound evangelical," a succession of chance events, impulsive actions, and wrong decisions compromise Cole's integrity, expose the blindness of his romantic idealism, and undercut his inherited cowboy mythology's ability to account for either his experiences or the world itself.

Whether facing the world as an orphaned nomad or a prisoner, Cole discovers his cognitive map of the world has become decisively altered by inscrutable forces of change and his personal involvement in the death, chaos, and anarchy of Chapter Three. Events thus position him in a liminal space betwixt and between established and emergent ideas, values, meanings, and identities. About the Saltillo prison, Rawlins says "I never knowed there was such a place as this"; about his killing in self-defense of the *cuchillero*, Cole states "I never thought I'd do that"(215). As a result, the chapter's events do not so much dramatize Cole's struggles to sustain his idealism in the face of the horrific events assaulting his body and spirit. Rather, they begin to cure him of his sentiments, to paraphrase Alfonsa's words, and thus force a pragmatic reassessment of his idealism. Rawlins will justify Cole's killing another man by appealing to the logic of self-defense and the determinism of fate. Cole, however, replies "You dont need to try and make it right. It is what it is"(215).

Cole's sententious response clearly discloses his emergent understanding of the crucial difference between maps (rationalizations and justifications) and the country itself ("It is what it is"). He intuitively understands that the full nature of "it" lies outside or beyond the web of words always constructed by desires and ideals. And that while such webs or maps certainly are necessary to survive in the world, they can only represent provisional, contingent truths and they serve, like Cole's performance as a horsebreaker, to remove us from the world's "resonance." Cole's comment reveals his newfound commitment to the practical, material effects of thinking and action and his readiness to assume full responsibility for his actions.

In jail or prison, Cole traverses a literal and metaphorical borderland space in which dream and reality, order and chaos, life and death, myth and history, and idealism and pragmatism intersect and inhabit each other just as the "lights from the cafe and from the lamps in the plaza" of Saltillo are said to "lay bleeding in the black pools of water"(210). Another way to gauge what Cole learns or how his character develops as Chapter Three concludes is to consider the matrix created by McCarthy's repetitive sounding of the words *blood, red* (and the neologism *bloodred*), *bleeding,* and *burning*. With the exception of the novel's evocative final paragraph, this matrix of words, along with its affiliated imagery of the heart, culminate in Chapter Three's image of the blossoming "red boutonniere" and the "fan of bright arterial blood" spurting from the blue shirt of the *cuchillero* whom Cole stabs in the heart (201). "Blood" literally represents a pulsing fluid without which life cannot exist, and it metaphorically signifies the life and instinctual force of passion and desire. As this death scene suggests, "blood" imagery also discloses McCarthy's *dialectical* (rather than dualistic) vision of existence. Keyed by the novel's repetitive association of "bloodred" with sunrise as well as sunset moments, the metaphor here of "blood" as both a blossoming flower and sign of fading life forwards the ambiguous unity in opposition of beginnings and ends, creation and destruction, beauty and pain in McCarthy's fiction. Moreover, as this death scene illustrates, "blood" importantly connotes a Dionysian violence, how passion embodies an elemental desire for power and mastery. The uneven, often extravagant coursing of "blood" cannot finally be controlled or appeased by laws, codes, ritual codes, abstract reasoning. This of course is the "lesson" Don Hectór conveys to Cole with his allusions to *Don Quixote* while they play pool in Chapter Two, it is essentially one of the "truths" Perez relays to Cole in the Saltillo prison, and, rephrased by Alfonsa in chapter four as "the love of blood," it represents a "constant in history" that even God "seems powerless to change"(239).

When Cole looks "deep" into the *cuchillero's* eyes, he recognizes a "whole malign history burning cold and remote and black"(200). As it dawns on him that he might die in this prison, Cole falls from innocence into experience through the shedding of his and others' "blood." By recognizing the depths of history's malign "love of blood" in the *cuchillero's* eyes, Cole also begins to understand the vacuousness of placing—as he learns the Madero brothers did during the Mexican Revolution—any "trust in the basic goodness of humankind"(237). Dramatizing Cole's belated recognition of a "malign" history's existence, Chapter Three establishes Cole's nascent awareness of both the random, contingent, and provisional nature of human truths and the inherent limits "blood" imposes on one's will and heart's desire. When Cole and Rawlins leave Texas they are said to ride like "thieves" with "ten thousand worlds for the choosing"; by contrast, in the Saltillo prison Perez informs Cole that the Mexican authorities are waiting to "choose" the crime with which to charge him and Rawlins (193). Perez's comment reinforces Cole's hard-earned awareness of the role power plays in authorizing just "who gets to say" what are truths and lies (see 137; 168). More importantly, the verbal parallelism provided by the repetition of "choosing" in these passages indicates that "the love of blood" in history has occurred and occurs *both* in Texas *and* in Mexico. In the novel's second scene, the narrator envisions a Comanche nation "lost to all history and remembrance." In Chapter Three Cole's visual epiphany regarding the "whole malign history" and his personal immersion in its "love of blood" readies him — and the reader — to understand how the mythic ranching life he desires to relive is underwritten by a "history" of dispossession and violence that transcends national borders, uniting the lost ranch in Texas with the lost paradise of La Purísima in Mexico.

CHAPTER FOUR

In the end we all come to be cured of our sentiments. Those whom life does not cure death will. The world is quite ruthless in selecting between the dream and the reality, even where we will not. Between the wish and the thing the world lies waiting.

(238)

The six sections of Chapter Four dramatize the journeys in John Grady Cole's life between the early fall of 1950, when he returns to La Purísima, and March 1951, when the novel ends with him at sunset riding across the Pecos River at Iraan, Texas, heading west "into the darkening land, the world to come"(302). After his initial journey northward from Saltillo to La Purísima, Cole travels south to Zacatecas to meet and, ultimately, say farewell to Alejandra. He then reverses the journey south made in Chapter One, traveling north through Coahuila and, after another encounter with the Mexican captain at Encantada, he eventually crosses the Rio Grande and re-enters Texas on a cold, gray Thanksgiving Day, riding Redbo and driving before him Rawlins's horse Junior and Blevins's bay horse.

Just as the supposed "paradise" of Chapter Two structurally counterpoints the "purgatory" of Chapter Three, so too the details, images, and scenes of Cole's journeys in Chapter Four balance and mirror those features in Chapter One's portrayal of his journey south into Mexico. To cite a few examples: his final departure from La Purísima and farewell to Alejandra echo the first chapter's portrayal of his departure from family and (ex)girlfriend in Texas, while the funeral of his *abuela* in the novel's penultimate scene parallels his grandfather's funeral in the novel's second scene. The Ozona courtroom scene where title to the bay horse is contested and Cole's later visit to the judge's house balance the earlier scenes where Cole talks with a lawyer and his father about the property right to his grandfather's ranch. In both opening and closing chapters Cole is chased by a posse of men from Encantada; in both chapters Cole at some point travels through snowstorms. Searching at novel's end, like Coleridge's Ancient Mariner, to rid himself of the "millstone" of the dead Blevins's bay horse, Cole's visit to the radio preacher Jimmy Blevins in Del Rio, Texas, balances with the opening chapter's conversation about the evangelist's radio show and its introduction of the mysterious thirteen-year-old who has assumed the preacher's name. The novel's concluding image of Cole riding west into a "bloodred sunset" while Indians watch from a distance echoes the first chapter's lyric description of Cole and the Comanche ghost nation at sunset jointly riding the western fork of the track bearing south from Kiowa country (for more on the chapter's structure see the Gail Morrison essay cited in chapter five).

As has been the case throughout the novel, McCarthy's parallelism of scenes and repetition of images and motifs reinforce the novel's themes and clarify the changes in Cole's character during his ritual passage from innocence into experience. The dramatic change in the novel's tonal presentation of Cole's opening and closing journeys is underlined by the implicit contrast between Cole's mother's clipped, patronizing comments and by Alfonsa's involved story about her past and the Mexican Revolution and the structural counterpointing of Cole's insensitive farewell to Mary Catherine with his tortured goodbye to Alejandra. Whereas the young cowboys who steal away from Rawlins's home at the novel's outset are likened to "young thieves in a glowing orchard," when Cole returns to La Purísima early in Chapter Four he rides through an orchard and bites into an apple that "was hard and green and bitter"(226). Whereas the trio of American horsemen exuberantly gallop their horses after crossing the Rio Grande under a quarter moon on a warm night, a "pale and shivering" Cole crosses back into Texas and sits his horse in the falling rain, weeping as he thinks of his dead father. Whereas in earlier scenes — as the discussion of Chapters Two and Three has highlighted — Cole places his hands to turn "dead center" to the earth or to grip the roof of a truck cab "like a newfound evangelical," at his *abuela's* gravesite, by contrast, he turns "his wet face to the wind and for a moment he held out his hands as if to steady himself or as if to bless the ground there or perhaps as if to slow the world that was rushing away and seemed to care nothing for the old or the young or rich or poor or dark or pale or he or she"(301).

In Chapter One, when Rawlins asks him whether he ever got "ill at ease," Cole laconically responds "sometimes," adding that one probably should feel ill at ease "if you're someplace you aint supposed to be"(37). In Chapter Four, in response to Rawlins' comment that he ought to stick around the "still good country" around San Angelo, Cole answers "I know it is. But it aint my country." Asked then by Rawlins where his country is located, Cole replies "I dont know where it is. I dont know what happens to country"(299).

As this scene and the above examples of McCarthy's structural counterpointing of image and scene suggest, "what happens to country" (the theme of incessant historical change and loss) has chastened Cole's character, basically "cured" him of his sentiments by novel's end, leaving him "ill at ease" in "someplace" he now does not believe he is "supposed to be" (the theme of alienation and exile). Besides humbly knowing that he no longer has a home and that he doesn't know "what happens to country," though, what has Cole learned as his rite of passage proceeds through its final stages? Furthermore, as the chapter's events lead him to understand his self-proclaimed condition of exile, how should we understand or define his emergent task in the wake of the series of deaths and losses he has experienced?

What is arguably the most crucial instance of McCarthy's method of structural counterpointing in Chapter Four provides a convenient way to begin answering such questions. When Rawlins somewhat miraculously shoots a buck during their opening journey south, Cole simply says that it was "a hell of a shot"(90). As they eat the cooked venison, Rawlins recollects seeing vaqueros hang the thinly sliced meat of a heifer on poles around a fire so that at night, when one looked through the thin red sheets of curing meat, it "was like lookin through somethin and seein its heart"(91). During Cole's final journey northward, however, the parallel scene in which he shoots a small doe elaborates a fuller emotional response that, among other things, transforms Rawlins's descriptive heart image into one with interpretive meaning. After shooting the doe, Cole kneels in supplication beside the animal, touches her neck, and watches her eyes as the moment of death arrives. In fact, he continues "watching her for a long time" and thinks about the Mexican captain, Blevins, his first vision of Alejandra, and "the cold blue cast" to the dead deer's eyes that announced the animal's transition into "but one thing more," like the grass, blood, and stone she "lay among in that darkening landscape"(282). Thinking about the dead animal's cold blue eyes triggers another remembrance of Alejandra "and the sadness he'd first seen in the slope of her shoulders which he'd presumed to understand and of which he knew nothing and he felt a loneliness he'd not known since he was a child and he felt wholly alien to the world although he loved it still. He thought that in the beauty of the world were hid a secret. He thought the world's heart beat at some terrible cost and that the world's pain and its beauty moved in a relationship of diverging equity and that in this headlong deficit the blood of multitudes might ultimately be exacted for the vision of a single flower"(282).

The passage's allusions to "pain" and "sadness" connect Cole's recognition of the "secret" hidden in the world's "heart" to the chapter's earlier scenes at Zacatecas where Alejandra finally declares she cannot forsake her father's love or renege on her promise (to Alfonsa) to refuse Cole's suit. In Chapter Three Cole drives a switchblade into a man's heart; in Zacatecas, however, after Alejandra's rejection, Cole experiences agony "like a stake" in his heart. Foreshadowing his reflections when he kneels beside the dead doe, in Zacatecas he ruefully realizes his ignorance and the hollowness of his presumptions. Even if he can now rightly presume to know what circumstances could make one liable to pain's "visitations," what he hadn't known before was that this world's mindless "pain" — "some formless parasitic being seeking out the warmth of human souls" — "had no way to know the limits of those souls and what he feared was that there might be no limits"(256–57).

Cole's emergent knowledge of pain's immense possibilities and, by contrast, of human cognition's limits suggests he has fully internalized Perez's lessons about evil's material existence and about the "false impressions" resulting from the belief that humans control either themselves or their world (195). Secondly, his epiphany about the world's "secret" — how pain, blood, and sacrifice underpin its evanescent beauty—suggests he now has internalized the various truths conveyed to him by Don Hectór and, most importantly, by Alfonsa during her recounting of her own and Mexico's violent history. The impact of these lessons, reaffirmed in Chapter Four by Cole's dream of "the order in the horse's heart" and by Alfonsa's storytelling, reinforces how the Saltillo prison world basically represents only a cruder embodiment of the larger society's materialism, class hierarchies, and competitive individualism. Cole's belated recognition of the utter difference between the truths of nature and those constructed by desiring humans culminates with his sense of the "diverging equity" of pain and beauty in the world's elemental economy. Thirdly, besides revealing his growing ability to mourn, Cole's physical gestures and meditative response to the deer's death suggest his understanding of his complicity in events and his readiness to assume responsibility for the consequences of his actions. The scene of the doe's death, then, foreshadows Cole's eventual "naming of responsibility" (Alfonsa's phrase) when he confesses to the judge that "I was the one that brought it about. Nobody but me"(291).

While generally admiring McCarthy's portrayal of Alfonsa's complex, if not contradictory character, critics have disagreed about whether she represents a symbolic serpent whose action expels the lovers from the "paradise" of La Purísima or Cole's most perceptive mentor. Certainly, the elements of her long story about her family's history through the Mexican Revolution—a father's interdiction against a love affair; the failure of idealism and a loss of innocence; betrayal and bloodshed—illustrate how her panoramic history connects with and determines present circumstances at La Purísima as much as does the more immediate matter of Blevins's horse and crimes. Her history—entwined with that of the Madero brothers—uncannily anticipates and mirrors the affair between Alejandra and Cole. Like Gustavo, Cole seems to Alfonsa to be one of those people to whom "circumstances" conspire against, regardless of best intentions and ideals; and like Gustavo, who honors Alfonsa after her shooting accident by conversing frankly with her about the place of misfortune in the world, Alfonsa tutors Cole about the way the world's life and death ultimately "cures" everyone of "sentiments." While recollecting Gustavo's comments, Alfonsa indirectly defines what will become Cole's true task: to become "a person of value" in the world. For Alfonsa, authentic value cannot be subject to "the hazards of fortune"(235). A "person of value" ultimately will see and honor "what is true above what is useful" or expedient— and "true," Alfonsa adds, means "what is so" not what is "righteous."

As events force Cole to discard his nostalgic myth of the cowboy and cure him of his dogmatic idealism, he incrementally learns to see "what is so" rather than predominantly to project the "real world" as a "dream withal." This task requires courage, and Alfonsa reminds him that the courage to see and value "what is so" entails regarding "courage" as a "form of constancy": "it was always himself that the coward abandoned first. After this all other betrayals came easily"(235). Courage; responsibility, loyalty; forging a pragmatic orientation toward provisional human truths; understanding that while the "connectedness of things" may be real, things also reveal "endless" origins or causes which "enact the deaths of great men in violence and madness"(230–31)—such values and beliefs voiced by Alfonsa are put into action when Cole acts to recover Redbo, Junior, and Blevins's bay horse and gains retribution for Blevins's death. Gustavo tells Alfonsa that the "gift" misfortune bestows is in fact that of seeing "what is so" in the world—seeing it "right." While possessing the courage to see the world "right" without the blinders of sentiment, dogma, or myth, however, those who have endured misfortune have yet to "make their way back into the common enterprise of man for without they do so it cannot go forward and they themselves will wither in bitterness"(235). Like his father whose "sunken eyes" look out at an "altered" or "suspect" world in the wake of his military service, Cole begins to "see it right at last" as he enters manhood (23); but unlike his father, Cole's ability to still "love" this "alien" world and his successful retribution for Blevins's death confirms how, in the end, his string of losses and felt knowledge of the wheeling world's indifference result in neither despair nor bitter cynicism nor his nostalgic withdrawal from the world.

The novel's final scene depicts Cole heading further west in quest of his "country" and the rightful owner of Blevins's horse, the "bloodred" sun "coppering his face" and creating a single long shadow of him aboard Redbo and the trailing bay horse (302). He is "lighting out for the territory" again, but unlike Huck Finn he understands he cannot escape or transcend history and its "love of blood." Having been cured of his "sentiments," the orphaned Cole, as he was in the novel's opening scenes, occupies once again a liminal space between a lost mythic past and an uncertain "world to come." The final scene unifies several of the novel's major color images and motifs — red shades and tones; sunset; desert; shadows — and Cole's being watched by the Comanche nation's descendants produces, like the narrator's rendition of his first sunset ride on the Comanche trail, a flickering spectral effect — as if his history were haunted (as indeed it has been) by the ghosts of others. Just as the novel's first image of Cole is that of his reflection in a flower vase, so its final image of him is of his *shadow* passing and vanishing "into the darkening land."

Such references and images of passing, of the color red, and sunset in the west, and the sight of a solitary bull writhing in the dust "in sacrificial torment" promote the passage's elegiac tone and rhythm. As McCarthy envisions the scene, then, its rather mundane series of actions and sights (pumpjacks; a bull; a horseback ride; wind at sunset) get encrusted with mysterious, logically unrelated

elements and similes. Along with the passage's serial grammar (successive clauses combined by "and"), McCarthy's method here pro-
motes sheer adjacency (proximity or juxtaposition) and dispersal:
Allusions to red, sunset, darkness, and long shadows emphasize
transience and horizontal motion instead of congealing into meta-
phors suggesting organic growth or decay.

This imaginative handling of form and content in the novel's
final scene has a twofold effect. For one thing, McCarthy's method
flattens out things and situates them in some egalitarian foreground
plane where the dust powdering a horse's legs is just as significant
as a human whose heels touch a horse. Not transcendence or
salvation through faith or grace, then, but a secular, operational
idea of truth as verified through specific practices and contexts is
stressed. In addition, McCarthy's vision fosters an ambiguity and
irresolution through its simultaneous invocation and subversion of
the traditional western's formulaic ending calling for the capable
hero to ride into the sunset after delivering the community from its
oppressors.

The novel's final scene keys this ambiguity and irresolution to
the image of the solitary bull writhing in "sacrificial torment." Bulls
are among the four things that Alfonsa says Spaniards will not
believe in unless they can "be made to bleed"(230). Cole, too,
recognizes the world's "secret" reality centers on the exchange of
"the blood of multitudes" for a single flower's beauty. All sacrificial
acts contain an inherent ambiguity: the desired redemption depends
on destruction and loss; the scapegoat figure is both a potent force
and a vulnerable victim. On one level, then, Cole's chance encounter with the writhing bull serves as an emblem for his condition and
predicament. He too has sacrificed and been "redeemed through
blood" during his journeys. But on another level, both the bull's
and Cole's shared isolation and "torment" deepen the novel's ambiguous stance about his having learned how to become "a person

of value": that is, it remains entirely uncertain as to whether "being pledged in blood and redeemable in blood only" will transfigure, as sacrifices are supposed to, either the sacrificial victim or the community. Still seeking purgation and release, still unable to determine either Blevins's real name or the rightful owner of the bay horse, Cole rides on into "the world to come," both a "fortunate boy"(206) and a man of "misfortune set apart from the world"(235).

The Novel's Reception

> *He [McCarthy] is moonshine whiskey, clear and raw and po-*
> *tent, in a world more accustomed to Lite Beer and Diet Coke.*
> — KURT TIDMORE, "LIGHTING OUT FOR THE TERRITORY,"
> *WASHINGTON POST* "BOOK WORLD"

All *the Pretty Horses* was published on May 11th, 1992.
Expectations about the novel, however, had already been height-
ened during the three weeks prior to its official publication date. At
the end of April, Richard Woodward made brief but favorable references to the novel as part of his featured interview with McCarthy
for the *New York Times Magazine.* Two glowing pre-publication
notices followed this publicity—extraordinary because of the national reach of the *New York Times* and because of McCarthy's
reclusion—from major newspapers in two different regions of the
country (the *Houston Chronicle*; New York's *Newsday*). Then, during the week prior to the novel's official publication, critics—in
some instances novelists themselves—for the nationally-circulated
USA Today and for major daily newspapers in Washington, D.C.,
Boston, Philadelphia, St. Louis, and St. Petersburg printed glowing

reviews, essentially recommending all readers put *All the Pretty Horses* on their "must read" lists. In the first week of the novel's publication, the *New York Times*, *Los Angeles Times*, *Chicago Sun-Times*, and the national magazines *Time* and *Newsweek* published positive notices. Then, in dramatic contrast to the fate of McCarthy's previous novels, *All the Pretty Horses* first appeared on the *New York Times* hardback national bestseller list approximately a month after its release. As the 1992 summer progressed, warm reviews of the novel began appearing in major Canadian newspapers, and when the British hardback edition was released by Picador in the early spring of 1993 major periodicals in the United Kingdom and Ireland published uniformly favorable reviews.

Headlines introducing some of these reviews succinctly illustrate both the favorable tenor of and the major themes associated with the novel's reception in both North America and the United Kingdom and Ireland: "Lighting Out for the Territory: Breakthrough for a Cult Novelist?" (*Chicago Sun-Times*); " 'Pretty Horses': American Perfection" (*Newsday*); "Old West Reborn in 20th Century" (*St. Louis Post-Dispatch*). The phrase "lighting out for the territory," drawn from the conclusion to Mark Twain's *The Adventures of Huckleberry Finn*, highlights how reviewers typically identified McCarthy's novel as a coming-of-age saga that not only begged comparison to Twain's classic novel, but also called to mind the heroic stories of Odysseus, Jason, and the medieval knights who quested after the Holy Grail. "American Perfection" captures the widely held judgment that McCarthy's first volume of "The Border Trilogy" constituted a quintessentially *American* adventure story. From this perspective the novel's youthful protagonists, suspenseful action, and detailed attention to the natural world importantly contributed to an "American" tradition of adventure writing exemplified by, say, Melville's *Moby-Dick*, Twain's *Huckleberry Finn*, Jack London's Yukon stories, Hemingway's Nick Adams fishing and hunting stories, and Jim Harrison's *Legends of the Fall*. Writing for *The Observer*, for instance, British critic John Banville claimed that McCarthy was "the finest action writer since Hemingway," while the *USA Today* critic declared *All the Pretty Horses* to be "surely one of the great American novels."

As these headlines also suggest, two additional themes emerged in the reviews published between the novel's initial release and the later publication of both the British hardback edition and the Vintage paperback edition. The headline "Old West Reborn in the 20th Century" declares in shorthand form how McCarthy was thought to have written "the great 20th-century Western" and to have redeemed that genre's cultural significance in the process. This third theme attending the novel's reception typically appeared when critics either stressed, as Gail Caudwell did in the *Boston Globe*, the novel's elegiac "hymn to a way of life and a land that no longer exist," or contrasted this novel's more complex, lyric exploration of the vanishing West to the writing of such genre stalwarts as Zane Grey, Louis L'Amour, and Larry McMurtry, whose bestselling western *Lonesome Dove* (1985) had appeared in the same year as McCarthy's revisionist *Blood Meridian*. Finally, as the headline word "breakthrough" suggests, reviewers characteristically regarded this novel, in comparison to McCarthy's earlier work, to be his "most accessible" novel yet. Although Richard Woodward's feature interview followed the title "Cormac McCarthy's Venomous Fiction," he concluded in the interview itself that the fictional adventure of John Grady Cole was "unusually sweet-tempered for him [McCarthy]."

Most critics agreed that the novel's relatively greater accessibility, besides possibly enhancing McCarthy's sales figures, could be traced to several features. McCarthy, for a change, had created a more likable cast of characters and had included a tender, though doomed love story. The novel frequently presented buoyant vernacular dialogue and humor, while its rather straightforward adventure plot was filled with exciting action sequences. Perhaps most significant of all, McCarthy's dramatization of John Grady Cole's adventures seemingly implied an ethical stance that mitigated the author's usual existential nihilism. Because the novel's major character was neither psychotic nor socially deviant, critics predicted McCarthy's general readership would grow in numbers. Moreover, as Geoff Dyer observed in Britain's *The Guardian*, "the great strength of the new novel is that the simmering pathology of McCarthy's world is itself defined by a morality that survives — and derives strength from — every assault upon it." That there arguably was "morality" in McCarthy's fictional world and that *All the Pretty Horses* was arguably a sunnier and more genial work prompted certain critics to wonder whether such features (much less the novel's continuing commercial success) would perhaps mystify or, in the end, alienate the heretofore small number of McCarthy's loyal readers. Still, even if a backlash against McCarthy materialized on the part of those readers wanting to preserve McCarthy's cult status, critics nevertheless predicted that *All the Pretty Horses* would stand as McCarthy's breakthrough work and thus, for better or worse, terminate his status as the best "unknown" writer of American fiction.

In support of these extraordinarily superlative remarks, reviewers typically pointed with deep admiration to McCarthy's mythopoetic presentation of horses and to his skill at narration. Singled out for attention on this score were the scenes where John Grady Cole and Lacey Rawlins break wild horses or are pursued by the men of Encantada after they help Jimmy Blevins recover his horse. With regard to McCarthy's characterization, the critics typically praised his rendering of John Grady Cole and Alfonsa, while those reviewers who remarked on the novel's *Huckleberry Finn*-like picaresque qualities also praised McCarthy's creation of Jimmy Blevins (indeed, a handful of reviewers, noting that Blevins's execution-style death in Chapter Three occurs offstage, hoped McCarthy would contrive a way to have him reappear in the trilogy's later volumes). Although a small number of critics felt the novel started too ponderously, most nevertheless agreed with the reviewer for the *Atlanta Journal & Constitution* that the novel becomes "a storyteller's tale in the highest sense, riveting in its detail and action, profound in its lessons" once Cole and Rawlins begin their journey south to Mexico. Still other reviewers argued that this familiar, straightforward "storyteller's tale" brought into greater relief McCarthy's unique literary talent at simultaneously presenting characters and situations on individual and archetypal or realistic and allegorical levels. Thus, Madison Smartt Bell argued in the *New York Times Book Review* that the novel's plot—a hybrid cross between *Lonesome Dove* and *Huckleberry Finn*—clarified how McCarthy's overall thematic vision remains both "deeper" than McMurtry's and "darker" than Twain's. Whether using phrasing like "profound lessons" or "deeper" and "darker" vision, reviewers typically explained McCarthy's distinctive achievement by remarking on his risk-taking prose style and to his original narrative voice's high-stakes thematic exploration of issues of life and death, honor and courage, loyalty and love, justice and vengeance, and pain and redemption.

Even in the most warmly favorable reviews, however, critics expressed certain reservations about three particular aspects of the novel. And on both sides of the Atlantic a handful of reviews entirely critical of the novel did appear in print. On the negative side, a few critics felt McCarthy's characterizations were pedestrian, awkwardly handled and even cliched at times. Although even the most grudging reviewer often acknowledged McCarthy's talent at depicting the camaraderie of men at work, his portrayal of women characters left something to be desired. Whereas critics usually regarded Alfonsa as a fully developed, compelling character, those few critics reviewing the novel negatively regarded her as a misplaced Henry James-type of babbling heroine. Her niece Alejandra, furthermore, seemed to be all hair, sweat, and tears during McCarthy's soap opera vision of her love affair with Cole. Furthermore, as one critic argued, the characterization of John Grady Cole himself was just too unbelievable, this callow sixteen-year-old cowboy James Bond figure who in quick succession advises Don Hector about his quarterhorse breeding program, beats Alfonsa at chess, momentarily wins the girl, manages to kill a hired assassin in prison, recovers his gear and horses in a running gun battle with several men, and then doctors his own bullet wound with a heated pistol barrel. Secondly, besides matters of characterization, a few critics also found McCarthy's prose style and the novel's format difficult to assess. Spanish dialogue appearing without translation, McCarthy's disregard for standard punctuation conventions (particularly commas, apostrophes, and quotation marks), his abstruse diction, and his frequent crash-and-burn stylistic passages reminded some of Faulkner's worst rhetorical excesses. Though most critics found (and continue to find) McCarthy's prose seductive and compelling, a few critics decided that his shrill, "all too writerly writing" too often overwhelmed the characters and events and drew undue attention to McCarthy's presence, not the story itself. Such readers judged the adolescent philosophizing of McCarthy's two young cowboys to be cliched; such readers regarded the narrator's metaphysical speculations as utterly at odds with the kinds of characters and events being presented.

When one combines such critiques with the additional negative response—again, by a only a handful of reviewers—to what seemed to a the final chapter's gratuitously violent action and incoherent final paragraphs, the result, according to Richard Ryan in the *Christian Science Monitor*, is "woefully meager literature," certainly not "one of the greatest American novels of this or any other time," as Geoff Dyer's concluded for *The Guardian*. Moreover, as John Sutherland observed in this vein for the (London) *Times Literary Supplement*, perhaps the result of McCarthy's labor should not even be regarded as "literature." Precisely because the novel displays "a kind of grudging quality to the writing, as if it cost the author a dollar a word, or he was spitting it out like squirts of tobacco," Sutherland asks, "is this literature, or just another efficient genre exercise in the worthy, but no more than worthy, tradition of Zane Grey?" If thought about as a "genre exercise" in the tradition of Zane Grey, *All the Pretty Horses* comes off then as a tiresome "boy meets girl-boy loses girl shoot-'em up," rather than the predominant critical view that the novel was indeed a sophisticated literary reworking of the popular western formula and its mythology. Believing that McCarthy, as Ryan phrased the situation, was more interested "in reworking adolescent adventure fantasies than in producing a template of actual experience," a few critics linked a critique of the novel's stereotypical plot with the limitations of the genre western to register a third critical reservation.

In his otherwise glowing review in the *San Francisco Chronicle*, Michael Upchurch concluded that the novel "is a boy's story sumptuously told—a sort of highbrow Zane Grey—but if tests of virile strength don't appeal to you, *All the Pretty Horses* is going to come up short." On the one hand, this observation foregrounds the fascinating issue about whether McCarthy's novels in general—and *All the Pretty Horses* in particular—represent fiction primarily of interest for *male* readers, young or old. Whether one rates the novel as an unliterary "genre exercise" or as "one of the greatest American novels of this or any other time," that is, is it truly the case that McCarthy's "The Border Trilogy" mostly appeals to a mostly indoor reading public who possess, as Dyer writes, "a stifled longing for a fiction of the outdoors"? And furthermore, is such "a stifled longing" not necessarily an "English" thing but rather a quintessentially "male" thing? As Catherine Bennett, Dyer's colleague at *The*

Guardian, wryly observed about the overall "warmth of response to McCarthy" as the first two volumes of the trilogy appeared, any one of McCarthy's novels wold make "the ideal Christmas present for the man who has done everything except grow up." A decade after the novel's publication, both the gendered nature of McCarthy's fiction and the gendered grounds of its appeal remain a provocative and important issue for critical debate by both academic and general readers. At the time of the novel's original release, though, those reviewers who characterized the novel as a "boy's story" usually hastened to add certain qualifications so readers would not assume negative connotations. Thus, even if *All the Pretty Horses* is best described as, say, a "boy's story sumptuously told," it nevertheless remains "a classic western" appropriate "for adult audiences" (*St. Petersburg Times*), one that ultimately possesses "serious implications for Americans at any age" (*Newsday*). And John Banville — who called McCarthy "the finest 'action' writer since Hemingway" — was also careful to say that that McCarthy "has none of Papa's masculist posturings, and little of his sentimentality."

On the other hand, Upchurch's "highbrow Zane Grey" tagline signals another central preoccupation of McCarthy's reviewers and critics for the past decade. Given a book whose basic plot remains difficult to summarize without, in Banville's words, "making it sound like a Clint Eastwood vehicle," what exactly accounts, then, for its magnetic power? What exactly warrants the numerous favorable comparison reviewers repeatedly made between it and the various works of Faulkner, Hemingway, Melville, Joyce, and Mark Twain? Of course, an answer to such questions can partly be found in the various critics' enumeration of the novel's appealing features: its ambitious existential themes, its story's epic historical reach, McCarthy's refusal to patronize Cole's character and his quest; the author's powerful imagining of human-animal relationships and the landscapes of the natural world. Despite the periodic disclaimers

certain critics have voiced about McCarthy's at times over-the-top
writing style, however, the most frequent answer to such questions
ultimately centers on McCarthy's utterly original voice and prose
style. It all comes down, in other words, to what novelist Saul
Bellow called in 1981 McCarthy's "absolutely overpowering use of
language, his life-giving and death-dealing sentences."

In contrast to those few critics who complained that McCarthy's
prose rivaled Faulkner's "worst excesses," the great majority of critics
and reviewers brought forward several key points about McCarthy's
prose style. One point is that McCarthy's basic indifference to standard grammatical conventions regarding apostrophes, quotation
marks, and commas has the intended effect of emphasizing the
stark presence of each and every word on the page. Stylistically
speaking, then, McCarthy's grammar and syntax work to stress his
corresponding thematic point that everything, whether on the landscape of the page or in the world beyond, finally *counts*. (Or, as his
narrator puts it in *The Crossing*, "the right and godmade sun" rises
every day "for all and without distinctions" [425].) One virtue of
McCarthy's style, to put the matter another way, is that it seriously
forces readers to pay attention at all times, no mean feat in an
everyday babbling and flowing world signified by the catchphrase
"24/7." Another point, as most of the reviewers who have discussed
stylistic matters agree, is that McCarthy's occasionally elaborate
syntax and elevated rhetoric not only should be admired as risky-
taking experiments with language and form. His poetic prose registers can and should be respected also because they for the most part
succeed in conveying to readers the sublime mystery of the world's
gathered beauty and horror, as well as to how the physical world
outstrips our human ability to name and master it. Finally, defend-
ers of McCarthy's ornate literary language point to how his lapidary,
at times majestic prose effectively counterpoints the dialogue and

descriptive sequences that typically rely on straight-ahead compound sentences and the hypnotic repetitions of words and sounds.

Taken together, then, the reviews of *All the Pretty Horses* at the time of its publication in North America and in the United Kingdom and Ireland overwhelmingly emphasize — in the course of summarizing the novel's basic themes and plot — its author's stylistic gifts and storytelling genius as these re-imagine our culture's quest romance and formula western literary traditions. Though a great number of the reviews and criticism do little more than summarize the plot, predictions are nevertheless made about McCarthy's achieving a much-deserved critical and commercial success with *All the Pretty Horses,* and pleasure is frequently expressed about the fact that readers can look forward to the next two volumes in McCarthy's trilogy. Most reviews liberally quote from the novel's passages — a sure sign of the intense interest his prose style has created. Whether fiction writers themselves, freelance critics and journalists, or staff writers, the novel's critics and reviewers during the first year or so after publication introduced, either in passing or as a substantial part of their remarks, several of the key issues and questions that academic critics have been discussing seriously and at length, now that all the volumes of the trilogy have been published. These issues and questions center now, as they did in 1992–93, on evaluating the place of the seemingly more accessible *All the Pretty Horses* in McCarthy's overall body of fiction; on the precise nature of McCarthy's indebtedness to such illustrious predecessors as Melville and Faulkner; on what may be called the "politics" of the novel's use of Spanish and its depiction of Mexico, its people and history; on the specific aspects of McCarthy's style and how these promote differing affective responses in readers; and, as mentioned above, on the issue of whether the novel's appeal is fundamentally limited to certain types of male readers.

The Novel's Performance

After having published two favorable reviews of *All the Pretty Horses* within the first month of its publication in May 1992, the *New York Times Book Review* editors included the novel in its "Bear in Mind" category that listed their recommendations of noteworthy books of the publishing season not yet appearing on the bestseller list. At the end of May, the *New York Times* additionally recommended the novel in its list of "Books for Vacation Reading." Then, on June 7th, 1992, approximately a month after its initial release, *All the Pretty Horses* debuted at number 15 on the *New York Times'* national hardback bestseller list. On the copyright page of copies sold during June 1992 Knopf revealed that *All the Pretty Horses* had been reprinted four times during May and was being reprinted, in only its second month of publication, for a sixth time. For the rest of the summer 1992 the novel continued its steady sales, ranking from week to week between 12th and 15th on this particular national bestseller list. Because of the novel's immediate and sustained critical and popular acclaim, Vintage International — like Knopf, another publishing arm of Random House — announced plans to reprint McCarthy's earlier novels *Suttree* (1979) and *Blood Meridian* (1985) in new paperback editions.

McCarthy's *All the Pretty Horses* disappeared from the bestseller list during the fall 1992 season, but continuing word-of-mouth recommendations and the late-November news of its receipt of the National Book Award for fiction propelled strong holiday season sales. The novel eventually returned to the *New York Times* national bestseller list in mid-January 1993 and continued on the list through April 18th, 1993. All told, during the first year of its release the novel had appeared on the list 21 times, achieving its highest ranking (9th) in January 1993. When *All the Pretty Horses* was named winner of the National Book Critics Circle award for fiction in March 1993, a month before the end of its run on the *New York Times* list, wire service reports indicated the novel was then in its *nineteenth* printing. By the end of the hardback edition's run in April 1993 the novel had been reprinted 22 times. Meanwhile, the hardback British edition of the novel published by Picador during the same spring made the bestselling list of *The Times* (London), where it was also reported that the entire first printing of 5,000 copies had quickly sold out.

In June 1993 Vintage International released the first paperback edition of *All the Pretty Horses*. This paperback edition of the novel appeared on the *New York Times*' best-seller list during the months of August and September 1993, while *Publisher's Weekly* magazine listed the novel for 43 weeks on its trade paperback edition bestseller list. A year later, undoubtedly triggered by the publication of *The Crossing*, the Vintage *All the Pretty Horses* was listed at number nine on the *USA Today* list. Interestingly, the novel's hardback edition also returned at this time (June 1994) to this national newspaper's bestseller list (at number 45). In its review of *The Crossing*, *Newsweek* magazine claimed that over the two-year period since its publication *All the Pretty Horses* had sold over 180,000 hardback copies and around 800,000 paperback copies. Moreover, the magazine reported that the novel's widespread success had prompted Knopf to order an astounding 200,000 copies for the first printing *The Crossing*. By any standards, these figures are amazing for a so-called "literary" western novel that one reviewer dubbed "a high-brow Zane Grey." And of course these are incredible figures for an author whose previous novels, as mentioned in this study's first chapter, had never sold more than 5,000 copies apiece.

For the rest of the decade, critical reviews of the other volumes in "The Border Trilogy" naturally diverted primary attention away from *All the Pretty Horses*. Still, the reviews of the later two novels from 1994 and 1998 invariably compared and contrasted all the trilogy's volumes, with most reviewers agreeing that *All the Pretty Horses* represented the trilogy's strongest achievement. Another measure of the novel's impact on McCarthy's career was the Book of the Month Club's decision to have both *The Crossing* and *Cities of the Plain* serve as "alternate" selections for its numerous members. The acclaim for *All the Pretty Horses* also prompted Vintage International to reprint *all* of McCarthy's earlier novels in new paperback editions. Toward the end of the 1990s both unabridged and abridged audio cassette and compact disc versions of the novel were produced (the abridged version narrated by well-known actor Brad Pitt). More recently, a new Vintage paperback edition of *All the Pretty Horses* was released to tie-in with the novel's film adaptation, which finally premiered on Christmas Day 2000. This movie tie-in edition occupied the paperback bestseller lists for a brief time during the winter months of 2001.

At present, in addition to the available Vintage paperback edition, the Everyman's Library has issued an affordable one-volume hardback edition of the entire border trilogy. As devoted McCarthy readers are aware, the very first printing of the first hardback edition of *All the Pretty Horses* has now become a valuable commodity in the book trade. Rare and used book stores, as well as internet auctions sites such as those for Ebay and Amazon.com, typically offer first edition/first printing hardback copies with dust jackets for anywhere between $150 and $400, depending on the book's condition. A rare signed first edition/first printing of the novel will easily fetch upwards of $700. Advanced reading copies that display McCarthy's signature will list anywhere from $400 and $600, while a special boxed edition containing a signed advance reading copy of *All the Pretty Horses* currently sells for more than $1,000.

AWARDS

As mentioned in chapter one, *All the Pretty Horses* was named recipient of two of the most prestigious literary awards available in the United States. On November 18th, 1992, the National Book Foundation, located in New York City, named the first volume of McCarthy's border trilogy the winner of the National Book Award for fiction. The award carried with it a $10,000 honorarium. Other finalists in the fiction category for the 1992 award were Robert Stone (*Outerbridge Reach*), Christina Garcia (*Dreaming in Cuban*), Dorothy Allison (*Bastard Out of Carolina*), and Edward P. Jones (*Lost in the City*). Judges for the award were Leonard Michaels, Toni Cade Bambara, Philip Caputo, John Leonard, and Joy Williams.

In January 1993 the National Book Critics Circle announced the finalists for its award in fiction. As was the case with the National Book Award group, both *All the Pretty Horses* and Robert Stone's *Outerbridge Reach* were named finalists. Completing the set of finalists were books by Randall Kenan (*Let the Dead Bury Their Dead and Other Stories*), Richard Price (*Clockers*), and Joyce Carol

Oates (*Black Water*). On the last day of February 1993 *All the Pretty Horses* was named the winner of the fiction award, its closest competition for the honor reportedly being Kenan's book of short stories. *All the Pretty Horses* was cited by the National Book Critics Circle for presenting "such classic American themes as the vanishing frontier and coming of age, relating this story in a prose of remarkable beauty that can range from the vernacular of Mark Twain to an almost Biblical majesty."

All the Pretty Horses was also a finalist for the 1993 Pulitzer Prize in fiction, but as it turned out, Robert Olen Butler's *A Good Scent from a Strange Mountain* was named that year's recipient. Also in April 1993, the Texas Institute of Letters awarded McCarthy's novel its Jesse H. Jones Award for best book of fiction published in 1992. Five years later this same organization bestowed its Lon Tinkle Award for Lifetime Literary Achievement on McCarthy.

FILM ADAPTATION

Given the cinematic qualities of McCarthy's prose and the novel's heady adventure story, much less its extraordinary popular acclaim, *All the Pretty Horses* would appear to be an ideal vehicle for a Hollywood film production. Certainly Mike Nichols and John Calley thought so: after the novel's publication they purchased the novel's movie rights for a reported six-figure sum. Shortly thereafter writer Ted Tally, Oscar-winner for his *The Silence of the Lambs* script, produced a 150 page screenplay that was faithful to the novel with the major exception that John Grady Cole and Lacey Rawlins would be men in their twenties, not teenagers. After Nichols eventually decided not to direct the film, he approached actor-director Billy Bob Thornton, who had his own breakthrough success with *Sling Blade* (1996), with the project. When Thornton agreed to direct *All the Pretty Horses,* Miramax, with whom Thornton had a three picture contract, signed on with Sony/Columbia to co-finance the film's $45 million budget and also handle its foreign distribution.

But it was not until early 1998, around the time of *Cities of the Plain* publication, when casting for the film was completed and production plans began in earnest. Matt Damon was awarded the part of John Grady Cole after Leonardo DiCaprio apparently withdrew his name from consideration. The role of Lacey Rawlins went to Henry Thomas, while Penelope Cruz was set to play Alejandra Rocha. Lucas Black, Thornton's young acting cohort from *Sling Blade,* was cast as Jimmy Blevins. Filming began in February 1999 and continued for 73 days in the Santa Fe and Las Vegas, New Mexico, areas as well as in San Antonio. Thornton's comprehensive assemblage of all the script's scenes came in with a running time of nearly four hours. Originally scheduled for release during the December 1999 holiday season, the two major studios underwriting the film rescheduled it for a possible spring 2000 release. But this announced premiere was delayed again. Though the film's producers publicly stated that a later fall/holiday release closer in time to the selection of film award nominees would better suit a movie originally projected as a *Dances With Wolves* type of epic western, the movie's delayed release was more likely the result of creative disagreements about the film's overall running time among Thornton, producers, and studio heads. In any case, during the summer of 2000 Thornton re-edited the film, reportedly producing four versions with variable running times. He and Miramax head Harvey Weinstein eventually agreed on the 1 hour and 57 minute version, which was finally released on Christmas Day 2000 on 1,483 screens in the United States and 100 screens in the United Kingdom.

Only about one in four reviewers found the film to be a satisfying achievement. Most reviewers recognized the difficulty of translating such a "writerly" novel as *All the Pretty Horses* to the screen. A handful of critics thought the film's problems—a weak love story; pretentious philosophizing; plot cliches—highlighted the basic weaknesses of the novel on which it was based. Lucas Black's performance as Jimmy Blevins was widely praised, and certain scenes—such as the horse breaking sequence and Cole's dreams of horses—were thought to capture the novel's special vision. Still, the consensus view was that the film, regardless of its compelling cinematography and fine musical scoring, moved at too leaden a pace, was too disjointed or even cryptic because of its truncated editing, and displayed a lack of romantic chemistry between Damon and Cruz. A few critics thought the film's problems could be traced to studio interference with Thornton's vision. Along with the problems created by the filmmakers' decision not to cut entire scenes but rather to trim time from all the scenes, the film adaptation displays two major problems. One problem centers on the difficulty of dramatizing a coming-of-age story when the main characters, well, have already come of age. The other problem, as the most perceptive critics of the film noted, follows on Thornton's and screenwriter Tally's overly reverent regard for the novel. In most cases, Hollywood filmmakers, in translating original literature to a visual medium, make changes that too often overly simplify the original work's thematic complexity or reduce its interpretive ambiguities. But this time around, Thornton's and writer Talley's faithfulness in presenting the novel's fatalistic romance and its stoic code of male honor apparently prevented the movie, ironically, from generating any emotional resonance with its viewers.

Further Reading and Discussion Questions

> *The ugly fact is that books are made out of books. The novel*
> *depends for its life on the novels that have been written.*
> — CORMAC MCCARTHY

Further reading: Fiction

Readers new to McCarthy's fiction who enjoyed *All the Pretty Horses*, should consider reading the remaining two volumes in "The Border Trilogy," *The Crossing* (1994) and *Cities of the Plain* (1998). Readers should be aware, however, that John Grady Cole does not re-appear in the trilogy until its final volume. But the opening section of *The Crossing* will particularly reward readers drawn to McCarthy's prose style. Centering on young New Mexican cowboy Billy Parham's doomed effort to return a trapped Mexican wolf to its homeland, this long section arguably displays the most sustained and powerful example of McCarthy's poetic prose storytelling. *Cities of the Plain*, which unites Parham and Cole in 1952 in a story that predominantly focuses on another of Cole's doomed romances, apparently originated as a screenplay during McCarthy's early years in El Paso. As is the case with *All the Pretty Horses*, critics are still in the process of evaluating this novel's achievement and sorting out its relationship to the themes and forms of the trilogy's other volumes. For readers who want to read on beyond "The Border Trilogy," McCarthy's revision of the presiding cultural myths about the American West in his first southwestern novel, *Blood Meridian* (1985), remains essential reading. Though clearly not to everyone's taste, this dark and complex bloody rewriting of the nineteenth-century historical novel of the frontier—its indebtedness to Shakespeare, Melville, Hawthorne, and James Fenimore Cooper everywhere in view—has clearly emerged as the leading McCarthy text in discussions by academic critics and scholars. Noted scholar-teacher Harold Bloom, for instance, admiringly discusses this novel in his *How to Read and Why* (2000), while Denis Donoghue devotes an excellent chapter to it in his *The Practice of Reading* (1998).

Readers who complete the southwestern borderland novels and who are curious about McCarthy's earlier novels set in the Appalachian South should find *Suttree* (1979) and *The Orchard Keeper* (1965) of particular interest. Also, since for McCarthy—as this chapter's epigraph reveals—the "life" anyone may discover in his books "depends" on "the novels that have been written," readers who enjoyed *All the Pretty Horses* may want to consider further reading in the fiction of writers who either have influenced his work or whose aesthetic vision and subjects are similar to his. In his 1992 interview with Richard Woodward for the *New York Times Magazine*, McCarthy included among the short list of writers he for one considers "good" the names Melville, Dostoyevsky, and Faulkner. As mentioned in this study's chapter one, these writers make his short list because they "deal with issues of life and death." Besides Melville's *Moby-Dick*, (reportedly his "favorite" book), Faulkner's *Go Down, Moses* (1942), which includes his great hunting story

"The Bear," the Nick Adams stories (e.g., "Big Two-Hearted River") in Hemingway's important collection *In Our Time* (1925), and Jim Harrison's acclaimed novella *Legends of the Fall* (1979) should interest readers enthralled by the themes, the adventure plot, and the varying stylistic registers of *All the Pretty Horses*.

Now that he is no longer "the best-kept secret in American letters," critics and reviewers regularly invoke McCarthy's name whenever they comment on more recent novels that are set in Appalachia or the Southwest and that involve hanks of lyric prose or present adventure sagas with gritty dialogue and graphic scenes of violence that rupture various characters' sentimental illusions about themselves and the world. With regard to southern settings, admirers of McCarthy's work should consider reading Charles Frazier's National Book Award-winning novel of the Civil War, *Cold Mountain* (1997), as well as William Gay's *Provinces of the Night* (2000). With regard to contemporary writers' re-visioning of the history and myths of the American West, Kent Haruf's *Plainsong* (1999) and Annie Proulx's *Close Range: Wyoming Stories* (1999) are examples of the most imaginative and provocative treatments of the rural American West and its history to have appeared in the past decade. Finally, James Carlos Blake has been labeled by one reviewer, in a comment that speaks not only to his literary talents but also to McCarthy's impact, as the "next" Cormac McCarthy for his series of historical novels and fictionalized biographies of such frontier characters as John Wesley Hardin, Bloody Bill Anderson, and Pancho Villa. Readers should consider Blake's highly praised *The Pistoleer* (1995) or his *Wildwood Boys: A Novel* (2000). Finally, though largely set on the Canadian plains, Guy Vanderhaeghe's award-winning *The Englishman's Boy* is an evocative, densely-textured novel that interweaves episodic stories about the cattle country with that of a struggling Hollywood screenwriter in stylistic registers evocative of McCarthy's work.

Secondary Reading: McCarthy's Biography

Because of McCarthy's refusal to publicize himself or his writing, most commentators on McCarthy — including this one — essentially depend on the same short list of sources for biographical and career information. Readers seeking further information about McCarthy's life and the trajectory of his writing career should consult: Richard B. Woodward, "Cormac McCarthy's Venomous Fiction," *New York Times Magazine*, 19 April 1992, 28–31 (as mentioned above, the only published interview with McCarthy to date); Robert L. Jarrett, *Cormac McCarthy* (New York: Twayne, 1997); Edwin T. Arnold and Dianne C. Luce, "Introduction," in *Perspectives on Cormac McCarthy*, ed. Arnold and Luce (Jackson: University Press of Mississippi, 1999); and Garry Wallace, "Meeting McCarthy," *The Southern Quarterly*, 30 (Summer 1992). 134–39. Secondary literature on McCarthy also includes a handful of interesting and often humorous journalistic pieces by writers making pilgrimages to El Paso to try to meet McCarthy and discover more about his past and present life. Along with the Wallace essay cited above, two of the better examples in this vein are Michael Hall, "Desperately Seeking Cormac," *Texas Monthly* (July 1998) and "The Knock at the Door," *Time* (6 June 1994).

Secondary Reading: Critical Studies of McCarthy

Scholarly assessments of McCarthy's writing began in earnest with the special summer 1992 number of *The Southern Quarterly*, edited by Edwin T. Arnold and Dianne C. Luce. The first full-length critical discussion of McCarthy's novels is Vereen Bell's valuable *The Achievement of Cormac McCarthy* (Baton Rouge: Louisiana State University Press, 1988). Given their publication dates, these particular studies concentrate on McCarthy's body of southern fiction, though the special number of *The Southern Quarterly* does include some preliminary critical coverage of *All the Pretty Horses*. Though limited, a good first word about the interaction of character and landscape in McCarthy's first border trilogy novel can be found in the contribution from Alan Cheuse. For an accessible critical interpretation of McCarthy's work that includes commentary on all the southwestern borderland novels excepting *Cities of the Plain*, see Robert Jarrett's volume on McCarthy in the Twayne United States Author series (cited above). As its title suggests, Barclay Owens's *Cormac McCarthy's Western Novels* (Tucson: University of Arizona Press, 2000) focuses on the novels from *Blood Meridian* through *Cities of the Plain*. It argues, among other things, that *All the Pretty Horses* represents McCarthy's "thematic shift away from atavistic violence and iconoclastic characters" of his earlier novels, thus inaugurating "a new period" in his career. Owens does not consider McCarthy a "postmodern" writer and works hard to fit the action and characters of *All the Pretty Horses* into the frame of a Joseph Campbell-type myth of the hero's "progress." For a concise, provocative discussion that alternatively argues McCarthy's border-land novels illustrate a "New West postmodern mapping," see Neil Campbell's "Introduction" to his *The Cultures of the American New West* (Chicago and London: Fitzroy Dearborn, 2000).

The first scholarly conference on McCarthy and his work was held in 1993 at Bellarmine College in Kentucky. In the wake of this conference "The Cormac McCarthy Society" was created, and for the past several years it has annually sponsored and organized national and, more recently, international conferences on McCarthy's writings. Readers interested in tracking scholarly criticism of *All the Pretty Horses* (as well as other McCarthy works) should begin with *Sacred Violence: A Reader's Companion to Cormac McCarthy*, edited by Wade Hall and Rick Wallach (El Paso: Texas Western Press, 1995). This volume, which includes selected essays from the

· very first McCarthy conference, includes three rewarding essays on
the border trilogy's first volume: Nancy Kreml's "Stylistic Variation
and Cognitive Constraint in *All the Pretty Horses*; Linda Townley
Woodson's "Deceiving the Will to Truth: The Semiotic Foundation
of *All the Pretty Horses*; and Dianne C. Luce's " 'When You Wake':
John Grady Cole's Heroism in *All the Pretty Horses*." The aforemen-
tioned *Perspectives on Cormac McCarthy* collection also includes
Gail Moore Morrison's extremely useful essay subtitled "John Grady
Cole's Expulsion from Paradise." Though the essays by Luce and
Morrison largely agree on the nature of Cole's heroism, reading
them together will provide readers with probing, yet contrasting
views on the meaning and significance of Alfonsa's character and
role in the novel.

Scholarly critical discussions of *All the Pretty Horses* over the past
decade tended initially to concentrate on the novel's characterization, structure, and style in order to establish its major thematic
concerns and its relationship both to other McCarthy novels and to
those of his literary influences. As mentioned in previous chapters
of this study, alternative views regarding whether *All the Pretty
Horses* represents a break with or a continuation of the earlier
novels' thematic vision and aesthetics have been and continue to be
aired. In addition, scholarly readers, often in the course of advanc-
ing different readings of the novel's final chapter, have begun de-
bating whether the novel ultimately supports or finally critiques and
revises the traditional popular western genre and its typical celebra-
tion of American "progress" through imperial conquest and possession of foreign "others." Thus, while an earlier issue interesting
McCarthy's critics was that of sorting out the novel's perspective on,
say, the question of free will and determinism, more recently the
issue of whether the novel betrays racist and sexist ideological un-
derpinnings has engaged critical readers influenced by theoretical
developments in cultural studies. Finally, while critical discussion

about two other key issues—the relationship between gender and genre; McCarthy's topographical imagination—is underway, much more critical work on these issues remains to be accomplished.

Readers interested in exploring alternative positions on such issues should begin by examining three items: editor Rich Wallach's recently-published collection of critical essays entitled *Myth—Legend—Dust: Critical Responses to Cormac McCarthy* (Manchester: Manchester University Press, 2001); Daniel Cooper Alarcon's *The Aztec Palimpsest: Mexico in the Modern Imagination* (Tucson: University of Arizona Press, 1997); and Sarah L. Spurgeon, " 'Pledged in Blood': Truth and Redemption in Cormac McCarthy's *All the Pretty Horses*," *Western American Literature* 34 (1999), 24–47. A good introduction to McCarthy's fiction that focuses on the issue of free will and determinism is Tom Pilkington's "Fate and Free Will on the American Frontier: Cormac McCarthy's Western Fiction," *Western American Literature*, 27 (1993), 311–22. For a discussion of McCarthy's topographical imagination see Campbell, cited above; Stephen Tatum, "Topographies of Transition in Western American Literature," *Western American Literature* 32 (1998), 310–52; and Susan Kollin's "Genre and the Geographies of Violence: Cormac McCarthy and the Contemporary Western," forthcoming in *Modern Fiction Studies*.

Finally, the most useful critical discussion of the novel's film adaptation published so far is Jim Kitses's "Bloodred Horizons," *Sight and Sound*, March 2001, 12–15.

Web Sites and Discussion Forum

Created in 1995, "The Cormac McCarthy Home Pages," the official website of "The Cormac McCarthy Society," is located at *www.cormacmccarthy.com*. In addition to including brief biographical information about McCarthy and his career, this excellent website provides information and "breaking news" about the Society's activities, a discussion forum for general readers and scholars, and invaluable translations of the Spanish passages in McCarthy's southwestern novels. In addition, readers conducting further research on McCarthy's writings will find invaluable the website's reproduction of Dianne C. Luce's full and updated bibliography of reviews and criticism of McCarthy's work.

Discussion Questions

Teachers and book group participants preparing discussions of *All the Pretty Horses* will also find helpful material on the novel and its background at Random House's "Reading Group Center" internet site located at www.randomhouse.com/vintage/read/horses/.

1. In the novel's second scene, Cole is described standing on the crest of a hill "like a man come to the end of something"(5). A few pages later the narrator describes Cole as sitting a horse "as if were he begot by malice or mischance into some queer land where horses never were he would have found them anyway"(23). What do such passages say about Cole's character and his predicament?

2. Why doesn't Rawlins want Jimmy Blevins to ride with them? Why do they let him join him? Why does Cole decide he can't go along with Rawlins's desire to leave Blevins at two different points along their journey?

3. How does McCarthy use descriptions of the landscape and the weather to forward character, plot, and theme? Consider the description of the distant lightning in the thunderclouds that will cause Blevins to lose his horse, gun, and clothes: "As if repairs were under way at some flawed place in the iron dark

of the world"(67). Do events in the novel argue that the world itself is "flawed" and chaotic, so that any meaningful order results from human action? Or is it the case that the world, like "order in the horse's heart" Cole dreams about in Chapter Four, is made into chaos and disorder by humans?

4. Given the novel's linkage of "paradise" imagery with La Purísima and the nature of Chapter Two's romance subplot, Cole has been described as a fallen Adam, tempted and expelled from the garden. Is this a fair assessment? Though Alejandra tells Cole he is "in trouble"(131), what evidence is there to suggest he is the tempter as well as the tempted?

5. Don Hectór tells Cole "Beware gentle knight. There is no greater monster than reason"(146). Alfonsa reminds him that scars "have the strange power to remind us that our past is real"(135). What do such statements mean? Why are events of the Mexican Revolution important to understanding the novel's plotting? Is Cole a "gentle knight" like Don Quixote?

6. In prison, Rawlins says their troubles are "[a]ll over a goddamned horse," whereas Cole says, "Horse had nothin to do with it"(185). Who or what is responsible for their troubles? Is Blevins to blame? What does Cole's response indicate about his maturing sense of responsibility?

7. Rawlins says that a "decision" was made before "ever dumb thing I ever done in my life"(79). Alfonsa gives Cole two different views of fate. Using the image of the coiner in a mint taking a slug from a tray, she describes her father's belief in the "the connectedness of things" and the "accessibility of origins"; using the image of a "puppet show," she forwards the idea of "endless" origins and unknown causes determining events (230–31). Which view on the relationship between fate and free will seem most relevant to the novel's sequence of events? Consider

Blevins's fate or Cole's knife fight with the *cuchillero* — what are the causes? Could these events have been avoided?

8. How do horses figure in the novel? What role do they play? What is the significance of Cole's dreams about horses?

9. Why does Cole decide to retrieve his horse? Do the events following on his return to Encantada in Chapter Four illustrate the truth of Alfonsa's remarks that "courage was a form of constancy" and that "the desire" [for courage] was the thing itself"(235)? Is John Grady Cole a hero? If so, what is the nature of his heroism?

10. Gustavo Madero tells Alfonsa that "those who have endured some misfortune will always be set apart but that it is just such misfortune which is their gift and which is their strength and that they must make their way back into the common enterprise of man for without they do so it cannot go forward and they themselves will wither in bitterness"(235). At novel's end, is Cole making his "way back into the common enterprise of man"? Is he withering "in bitterness" as a result of his adventure? Compare and contrast the opening and closing scenes involving his grandfather's and his *abuela's* funerals in discussing these questions.

11. Is *All the Pretty Horses* essentially a "boy's book" of interest only to male readers? Through the course of Cole's adventure what conception of masculinity does the novel forward? What in the end distinguishes Cole's code of conduct from Blevins's code of honor?

12. Crossing into Mexico in Chapter One the young American horsemen are described as "making for the alien shore like a party of marauders"(45). Fixing the Mexican captain's separated shoulder in Chapter Four Cole says his "family's been practicin medicine on Mexicans a hundred years"(278). Regardless of

the sophistication of its language and technique, does *All the Pretty Horses* basically rehearse the classic western's myth of regeneration through violence? Though Cole and Rawlins are surprised to discover the lack of electricity in the Mexican villages, does the novel show "history" on both sides of the border to be similar?

13. In the Saltillo prison, Cole's feet are described as leaving "cold wet tracks on the polished stones that sucked up and vanished like the tale of the world itself"(206). Waiting on the bus that will take them away from prison, Rawlins says "[a]ll my life I had the feelin that trouble was close at hand"(208). Do such lines embody McCarthy's overall vision of the world and the human condition?